D1360310

THE BOOK OF SAILING KNOTS

For Joseph Owen

THE BOOK OF
SAILING KNOTS

PETER OWEN

The Lyons Press

623.8882
OWE

Copyright © 1999 by Peter Owen

ALL RIGHTS RESERVED. No part of this book may be reproduced in any manner without the express written consent of the publisher, except in the case of brief excerpts in critical reviews and articles. All inquiries should be addressed to: The Lyons Press, 123 West 18 Street, New York, New York 10011.

Design and illustration by Peter Owen

Printed in the United States of America

10 9 8 7 6 5 4 3 2 1

Library of Congress Cataloging-in-Publication Data

Owen, Peter, 1950–
    The book of sailing knots / Peter Owen.
        p.   cm.
    Includes index.
    ISBN 1-55821-872-6 (pbk.)
    1. Knots and splices.   I. Title.
VM533.09424   1999
623.88'82—dc21   98-40920
                                                         CIP

Contents

INTRODUCTION

Sailing has undergone some revolutionary changes in recent years. It is now possible to navigate a craft using satellites and autopilots. Hulls are constructed from a variety of artificial materials, masts are made from aluminum, and rigging on modern-day yachts is almost entirely made of stainless steel. But the one component that has changed very little over time and is still totally necessary for any form of sailing or boating is the knot.

Sailing, like many other pursuits, has seen natural fiber ropes almost totally replaced by artificial fiber and wire ropes, but natural fiber ropes are still favored by some sailors and have distinct advantages, especially when it comes to decorative knotting.

The Book of Sailing Knots gives you the opportunity to master 50 classic sailing knots tied in rope. The knots have been restricted to those tied only in natural and artificial rope to devote each the space for clear instructions and meticulous step-by-step illustrations. Securing rope ends is also fully discussed.

The knots are divided into several distinct groups, each of which is used for different purposes. Practice is essential for good knot tying, so select the right knot for the job and practice until you are confident that you can tie it quickly and securely, in a flat calm or a storm force wind!

HISTORY

The art of knotting is as ancient as humankind. Stone Age people used knots to secure and fasten their traps, clothing, and housing; coiled and braided rope was found in the tomb of Tutankhamen; the Inca people of Peru used knotted string instead of written figures; and the Greeks, Romans, and other civilizations probably knew as much about knots as we do today.

It was, however, seamen and sailors, particularly those who served aboard the great sailing vessels of the eighteenth and nineteenth centuries, who exploited the full potential of knot tying both practically and decoratively.

The length of the voyages undertaken by sailing ships left sailors with little to do for much of the time; this was particularly true on whalers, which were at sea longer than other ships and were heavily overmanned. Isolated on board, unable for the most part to read and write, sailors had to find some way to fill their idle hours, and knotting was an ideal way of passing the time.

There was no shortage of raw materials. Sailing ships carried miles of rigging, and there was always a plentiful supply of spoiled rope (known as "junk") available for knotting. Sailors used their leisure hours to develop ways of tying knots that were both decorative and highly functional.

Knotting on board ship was often competitive, with secrets and intricacies of particular knots jealously guarded. Sailors were also responsible for many of the colorful descriptive names still given to particular sailing knots: the Turk's head (see page 122) and monkey's fist (see page 118), for example.

ROPES

R ope is manufactured in either natural or artificial fibers that can be twisted or braided and is available in a wide variety of sizes. Rope size can be measured by circumference or diameter or by a term; for example, twine, that tells you that it is a thin line for various uses.

Traditionally, rope was made by twisting fibers of natural materials together. The most commonly used materials were manila, sisal, coir, hemp, flax, and cotton. The fibers were twisted first into yarn, then into strands, and finally into rope, in a process called laying up. If you examine a piece of ordinary three-strand rope you will notice the strands go up and to the right, like a corkscrew. It has been "laid" right-handed. When the rope was made the fibers were twisted together to form right-hand yarn, the yarn was then twisted in the opposite direction to form left-hand strands, and these were twisted to form right-laid rope. If you uncoil one strand you can clearly see it is laid up left-handed, or twisted the opposite way to the whole rope. This is a vital principle of traditional rope making. Even with one strand removed, the other two strands cling together, leaving a groove where the missing strand should be. It is the alternate twisting that creates the tension that holds the rope together and gives it strength.

Three-strand natural fiber rope.

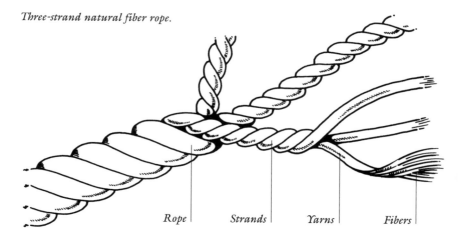

Rope | Strands | Yarns | Fibers |

NATURAL FIBER ROPE

For thousands of years, until shortages during World War II led to the development of man-made fibers, rope was made from natural materials—cotton and flax for manageability, coir and sisal for cheapness, manila and hemp for strength.

Natural fiber rope is normally three-strand and right laid. Four-strand, left-laid rope is much rarer and ten percent weaker—adding further strands does not increase strength. Cable-laid line (a nine-strand cable laid up left-handed from three-strand ropes) is 40 percent weaker than hawser-laid (three-strand) rope of the same diameter.

Natural fibers are only as long as the plant from which they were derived allows; the ends of these individual fibers (known as staples) are what gives natural rope its hairy, rough appearance. This gives them better traction and resistance than smooth man-made fibers. However, natural fibers have many disadvantages. They lack elasticity, and swell and become heavy when wet, making knots difficult to untie. They attract mildew and will rot if not stored properly, and they can be weakened and made brittle by strong sunlight, chemicals, and salt.

Nowadays, natural fiber rope is becoming less used in the sailing world, but for decorative purposes many still prefer vegetable fibers for their traditional appearance and the beauty of their natural colors and textures.

ARTIFICIAL FIBER ROPE

Artificial or synthetic materials have almost completely replaced natural fibers in the manufacture of rope. Man-made filaments can be spun to run the whole length of a line, do not vary in thickness, and do not have to be twisted together to make them cohere. This gives them superior strength.

Nylon, first produced in 1938 for domestic use, was the first man-made material to be used in this way. Since then a range of artificial ropes has been developed to meet different purposes, but they all share certain characteristics. Size for size they are lighter, stronger, and cheaper than their natural counterparts. They do not rot or mildew and are not affected by sea water. They are resistant to sunlight, chemicals, oil, gasoline, and most common solvents. They absorb less water than natural fiber ropes, and so their wet breaking strain remains constant. They can also be made in a range of colors.

Color-coded ropes for sailing make for instant recognition of lines of different function. In addition, artificial ropes have high tensile strength, are capable of absorbing shocks, and have excellent load-bearing qualities.

Nylon (Polyamide) fibers make ropes that are both strong and elastic, giving them outstanding capacity for absorbing shock loads. They are good for towing and, because they do not rot or float, they are particularly useful in sailing. One big advantage that sailors have found with this type of rope is that it is far more comfortable to hold and use than natural fiber rope.

Polyester (Dacron) ropes are nearly as strong as nylon and give very little stretch. They do not float and are highly resistant to wear and weathering. They are widely used in sailing for sheets and halyards. Polyester is also used in small sizes for twine.

Polypropylene (Polyethylene) is not as strong as nylon or polyester but it does make a good, inexpensive, all-purpose rope. Its one main advantage is that it is the only fiber that floats, thus making it particularly suitable for water-ski tow ropes and rescue lines. Floating does mean, however, that it may be caught in or cut by a propeller.

Because of their very nature, artificial ropes are constantly being developed and improved for a variety of different pursuits. It is always worth checking with your local chandler or specialist rope supplier about any new products that come onto the market for sailing and boating.

Braided artificial fiber rope

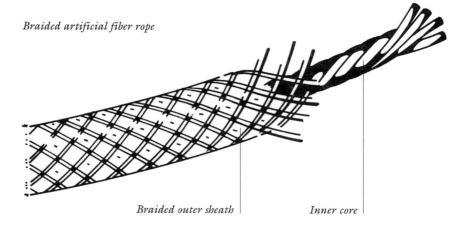

Braided outer sheath   *Inner core*

Twisted artificial fiber rope

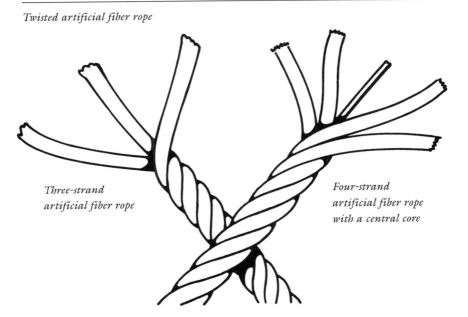

*Three-strand
artificial fiber rope*

*Four-strand
artificial fiber rope
with a central core*

Artificial fiber ropes do have some disadvantages, the main one being that they melt when heated. Even the friction generated when one rope rubs against another may be enough to cause damage, so it is vital to check your ropes regularly. Use plastic tubing to protect sections of artificial rope that you know will be subject to friction. It is also possible for heat friction to fuse knotted rope together so that it is impossible to untie the knot. Another disadvantage is that artificial ropes made of continuous filaments are so smooth that knots slip and come undone. Knots may need to be secured with additional knots or seized.

Artificial rope can be laid up or twisted like natural fiber rope or it can be formed into braided rope with an outer sheath of sixteen or more strands surrounding a central core that is either braided and hollow or made up of solid parallel, or slightly twisted, filaments. Braided rope is softer, more flexible, and quite a lot stronger.

Laid-up rope, made of thick multifilaments tightly twisted together, may be very resistant to wear but it may also be difficult to tie, and knots may not hold well. Do not buy a rope that is too stiff. Similarly, be wary of twisted rope that is very soft.

SHORTENING A ROPE OR LINE

The most successful and secure way to shorten a rope or line without cutting it is to use the **sheepshank**. The sheepshank is very much a sailor's knot and shares the special characteristics of other nautical knots in that it does not chafe, has a good jamming action, holds under tension, and unties easily.

Another important use of the sheepshank is the emergency repair of a damaged line. To remove the strain from the damaged section, tie a sheepshank, incorporating the weakened section in the middle of the knot. This will provide you with valuable time to make an effective repair or to replace the line.

The sheepshank

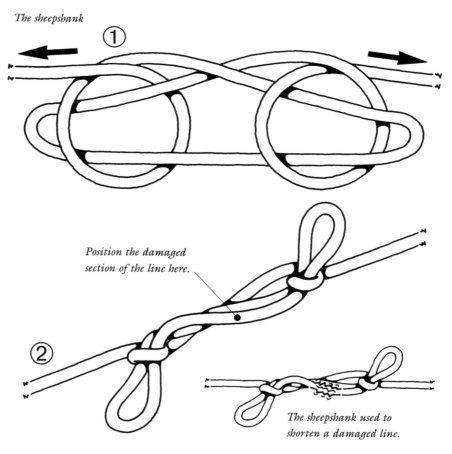

Position the damaged section of the line here.

The sheepshank used to shorten a damaged line.

LOOKING AFTER ROPE

Rope is sturdy material, but it is expensive, so it's worth looking after it properly. Caring for rope will help it keep its strength and prolong its life. Avoid dragging it over rough, sharp edges, or dirty, gritty surfaces where particles could get into the rope and damage it. Do not walk on rope or force it into harsh kinks. Inspect it regularly and wash off dirt, grit, and oil. Coil rope carefully and always make sure it is dry before coiling, even if it is artificial fiber rope. If it has been in sea water, rinse thoroughly to remove all salt deposits. At the end of the season, wash all ropes in a mild detergent, removing oil or tar stains with gasoline or trichloroethylene.

If knots are repeatedly tied in one section of rope, that section will weaken. The tighter the nip or the sharper the curve the greater the chances that the rope will break; if it does, it will part immediately outside the knot.

Finally, never use two ropes of different material together, because only the more rigid of the two will work under strain.

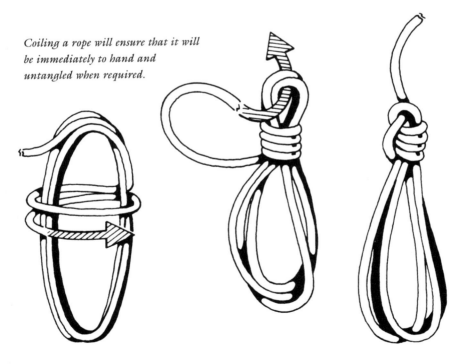

Coiling a rope will ensure that it will be immediately to hand and untangled when required.

CLEATING A LINE

A cleat is a deck fitting that is used to tie lines to on a temporary basis. The line is made fast to the cleat with a hitch. This particular hitch is often the first knot that prospective sailors come into contact with.

It is a simple but effective hitch, but it is also a hitch that many people tie incorrectly. It is easy to think that the more turns you put around a cleat the stronger the connection is going to be. This is not correct. If tied correctly, this hitch only requires a couple of turns to grip firmly and this also then makes it quicker to release.

Because lines have to be alternately made fast and quickly released as a matter of course in sailing, this is an important knot to learn.

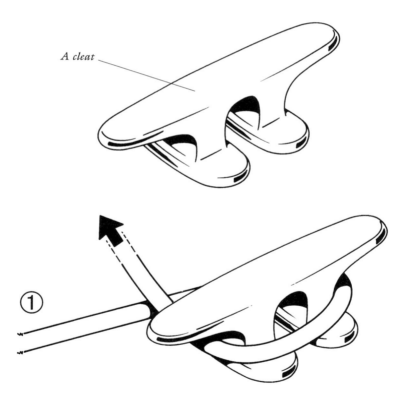

A cleat

①

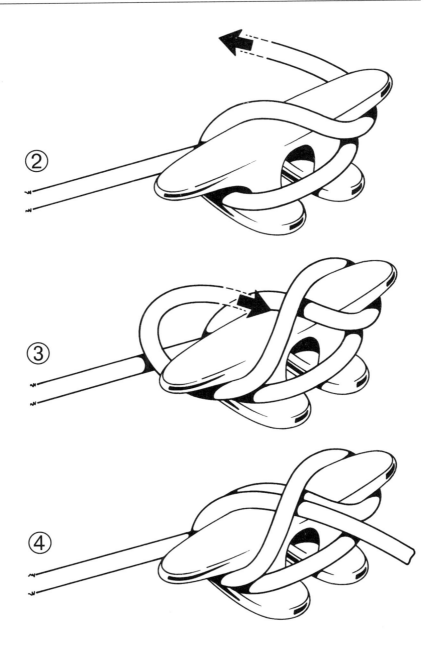

TOOLS

For the majority of sailing knots the only tool that will be required is a sharp implement to cut the rope or line. But the tying of a few knots can be made considerably easier by using some specialized tools. Because certain knot-tying tools are very specialized, they can only be obtained from chandlers or specialist sailing equipment suppliers.

A selection of the most useful tools and implements are featured here. If you have a particular knot-tying problem, contact your local chandler, who in most cases will be pleased to help you out.

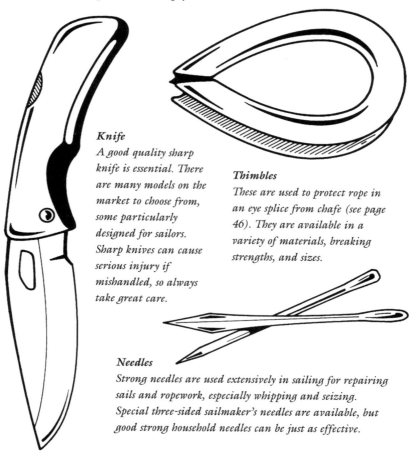

Knife
A good quality sharp knife is essential. There are many models on the market to choose from, some particularly designed for sailors. Sharp knives can cause serious injury if mishandled, so always take great care.

Thimbles
These are used to protect rope in an eye splice from chafe (see page 46). They are available in a variety of materials, breaking strengths, and sizes.

Needles
Strong needles are used extensively in sailing for repairing sails and ropework, especially whipping and seizing. Special three-sided sailmaker's needles are available, but good strong household needles can be just as effective.

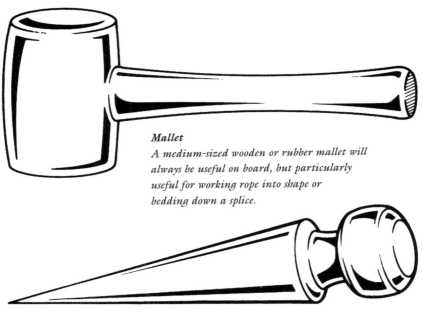

Mallet

A medium-sized wooden or rubber mallet will always be useful on board, but particularly useful for working rope into shape or bedding down a splice.

Fid

A fid is a sharp wooden spike used to splice or part twisted rope. It is made from hardwood and often has a decorative handle. Great care needs to be taken when using fids because, like knives, they can cause serious injury if mishandled.

Net Needle

These are made from wood or more commonly these days, plastic. Netting twine is wound on to the center of the needle, which is then used to create a net (see page 134). It is possible to make nets by hand, but to construct a good quality large net a net needle is vital.

How to Use This Book

The diagrams accompanying the descriptions of the knots are intended to be self-explanatory. Written instructions and special tying techniques and methods will accompany the more complex knots. There are arrows to show the directions in which you should push or pull the working ends of the rope or line. The dotted lines indicate intermediate positions of the rope. In many of the illustrations lines are shown faded out or cut short for clarity. When tying the knot you should always have a sufficient working end to complete the knot. The amount of working end required can often be calculated by looking at the illustration of the finished knot. Always follow the order shown of going over or under a length of line; reversing or changing this order could result in a completely different knot, which might well be unstable, unsafe, and insecure.

Rope Parts

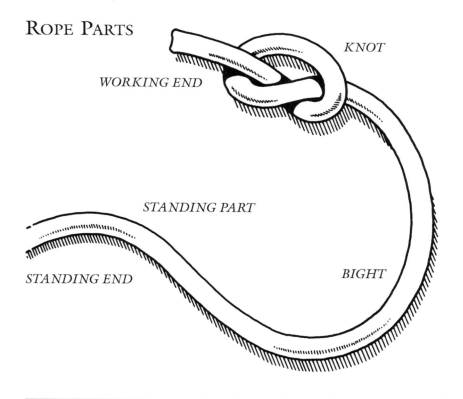

KNOT

WORKING END

STANDING PART

STANDING END

BIGHT

ROPE ENDS

A slowly unraveling rope with frayed ends is annoying, wasteful, and in some cases dangerous. But a rope with correctly sealed ends is safe, neat, and makes knots significantly easier to tie.

Artificial fiber ropes now are widely used in sailing and have many advantages, one of them being that the rope ends can be quickly and efficiently heat-sealed to prevent them from fraying. But natural fiber ropes are still used, and if left unseized, the ends will fray. A secure and easy way to prevent this is by whipping the ends. Use vegetable fiber twine or waxed polyester twine and always bind against the lay.

COMMON WHIPPING

This easily tied and practical whipping is, as its name suggests, one of the most widely used forms of whipping. But it should be remembered that if the rope end frequently becomes wet, most whipping twines will swell and stretch. This can lead to the whipping loosening and slipping off. So for rope ends that are subject to becoming wet, this should be seen as only a temporary whipping.

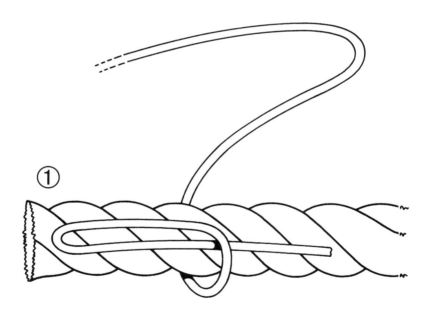

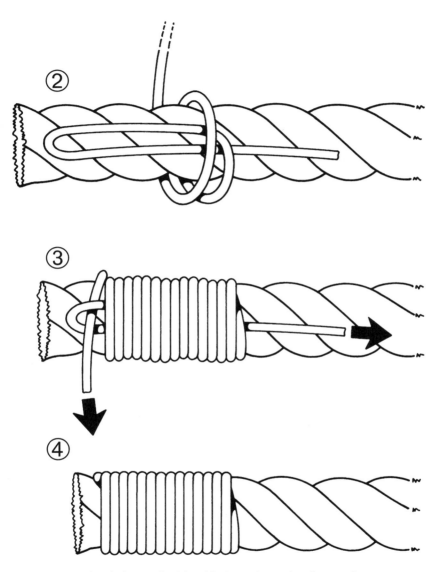

Trim the loose ends of the whipping twine and make neat the rope strand ends. With artificial ropes, the strand ends can be heat-sealed.

PALM-AND-NEEDLE WHIPPING

This durable and reliable whipping is especially suited to twisted natural fiber rope, but can also be tied on braided or artificial fiber ropes. It will stand up well to friction, so it can be employed for heavy usage. You will need a needle with an eye big enough to take whipping twine. Special sailmaker's needles are available for this purpose.

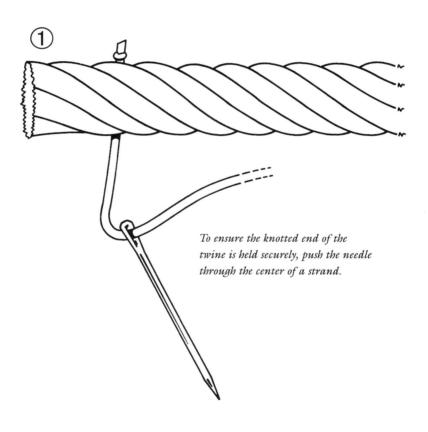

To ensure the knotted end of the twine is held securely, push the needle through the center of a strand.

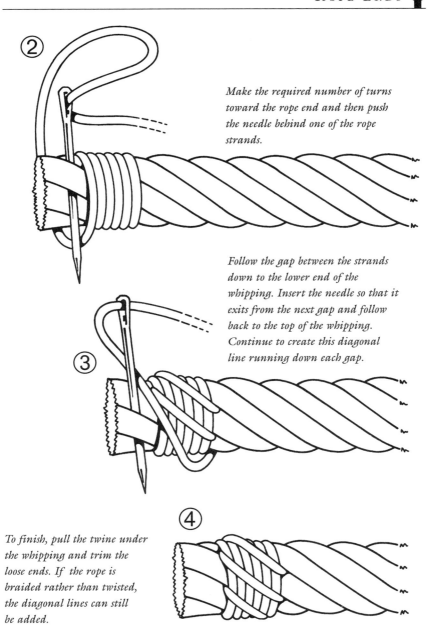

② Make the required number of turns toward the rope end and then push the needle behind one of the rope strands.

③ Follow the gap between the strands down to the lower end of the whipping. Insert the needle so that it exits from the next gap and follow back to the top of the whipping. Continue to create this diagonal line running down each gap.

④ To finish, pull the twine under the whipping and trim the loose ends. If the rope is braided rather than twisted, the diagonal lines can still be added.

SNAKED WHIPPING

This decorative and highly effective whipping is more suited to large-diameter ropes; it can prove difficult to tie on thinner ropes. It is important with all whipping, and especially snaked whipping, to make sure that each turn is pulled as tight as possible. Also, to make the snaking less likely to slip, as you pass the needle under the whipping, pick up a few fibers of the rope itself. The decorative appearance of this whipping makes it ideal for ropes that are left out on show or on board.

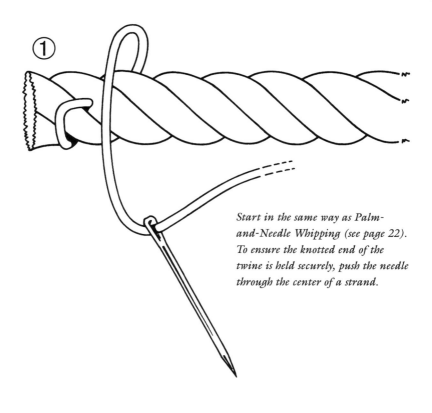

Start in the same way as Palm-and-Needle Whipping (see page 22). To ensure the knotted end of the twine is held securely, push the needle through the center of a strand.

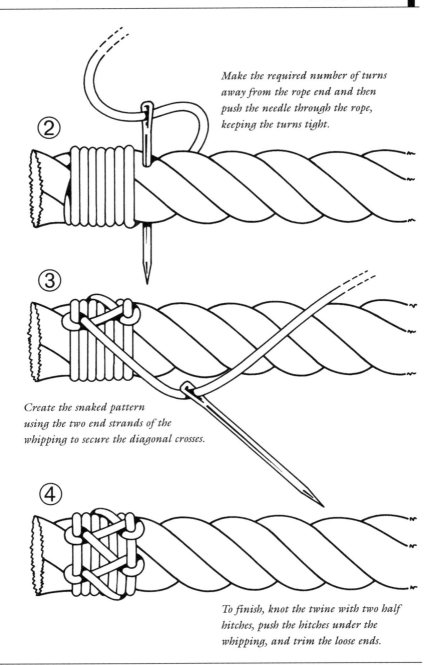

*Make the required number of turns
away from the rope end and then
push the needle through the rope,
keeping the turns tight.*

②

③

*Create the snaked pattern
using the two end strands of the
whipping to secure the diagonal crosses.*

④

*To finish, knot the twine with two half
hitches, push the hitches under the
whipping, and trim the loose ends.*

SEALING ENDS

Apart from whipping the ends of rope, there are three other options to consider to seal ends.

All synthetic rope ends can be sealed using heat. When you buy synthetic rope from a chandler they will cut it to the required length using an electrically heated knife, which gives a neat, sharp edge. When you cut synthetic rope yourself, use a sharp knife and then melt the end with a cigarette lighter or on an electric ring.

A quick and efficient method of creating a temporary seal is to use ordinary adhesive or electrical tape. And finally, on small stuff (any rope whose circumference is less than one inch), a simple stopper knot will provide an effective seal.

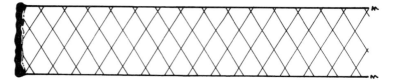

Heat-sealed synthetic rope

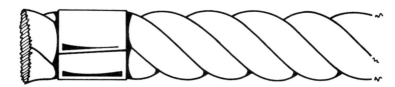

Rope sealed with adhesive or electrical tape

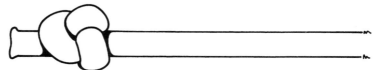

Rope sealed with a stopper knot

SEIZINGS

A seizing is used to bind two ropes together. The same thickness and type of twine or small stuff used for whipping is generally applicable for seizing.

Seizing can be used to bind two separate parts of rope together, but it is most widely used to bind the same piece of rope together to form an eye.

FLAT SEIZING

This simple form of seizing is good for light loads and to temporarily bind two pieces of rope together. For this type of seizing, use twine or thin line that has been prepared with a small eye at one end.

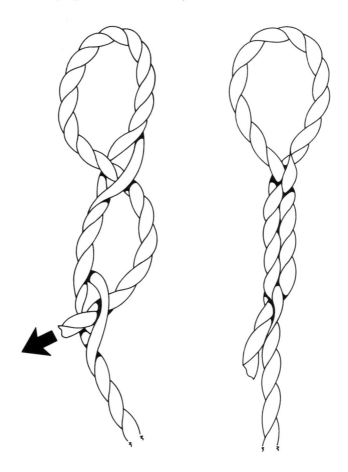

Prepare the seizing twine by forming a small eye in one end. This is done by opening up the strands and tucking the twine end through a couple of times.

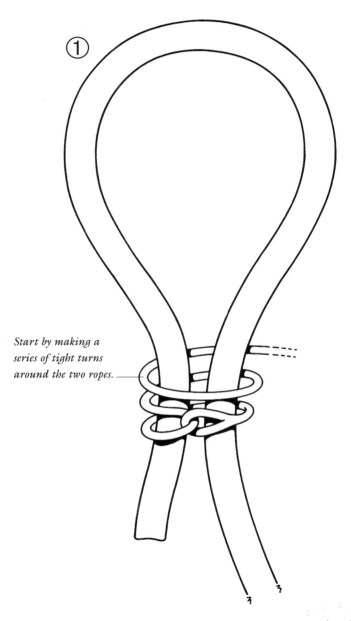

①

Start by making a
series of tight turns
around the two ropes.

continued on page 30

Flat seizing

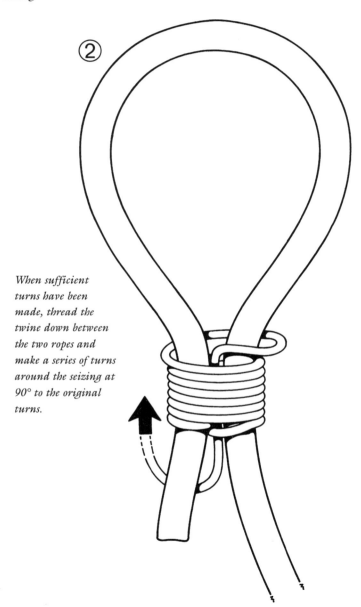

When sufficient
turns have been
made, thread the
twine down between
the two ropes and
make a series of turns
around the seizing at
90° to the original
turns.

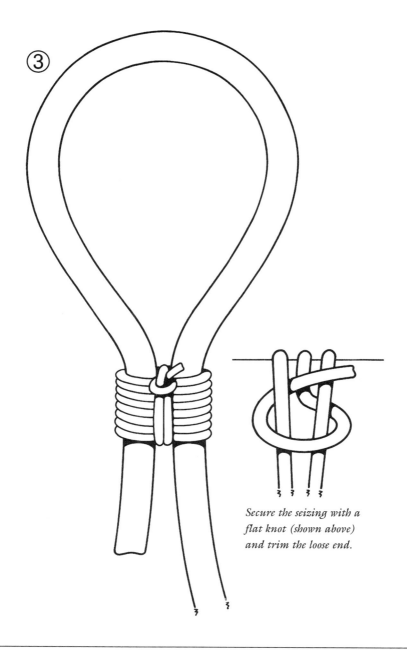

③

Secure the seizing with a
flat knot (shown above)
and trim the loose end.

PALM-AND-NEEDLE SEIZING

This method of seizing creates a strong grip on the rope, making it suitable for heavy loads. It is particularly useful for making eyes in the end of ropes. It is recommended that you use a sailmaker's needle to thread the twine through the rope.

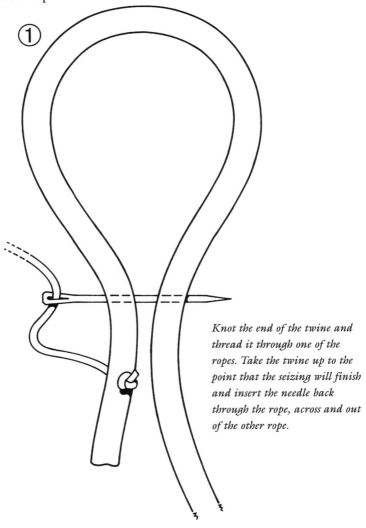

Knot the end of the twine and thread it through one of the ropes. Take the twine up to the point that the seizing will finish and insert the needle back through the rope, across and out of the other rope.

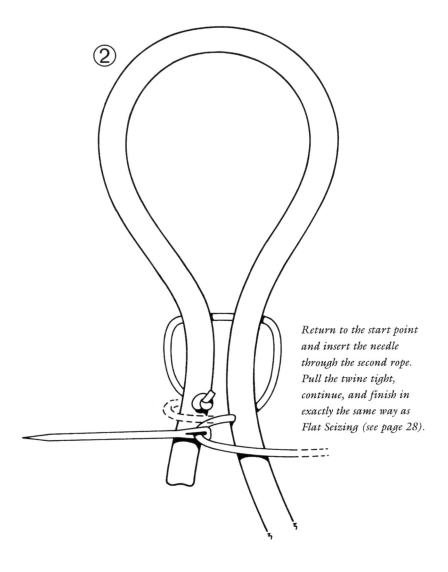

②

Return to the start point
and insert the needle
through the second rope.
Pull the twine tight,
continue, and finish in
exactly the same way as
Flat Seizing (see page 28).

Racking Seizing

This form of seizing should be used if the seized rope parts are to be subject to excessive, uneven, or sideways loading. Instead of making complete turns, thread the twine over and under the ropes. This will substantially strengthen the seizing. Racking can be applied to Flat Seizing (see page 28) and Palm-and-Needle Seizing (see page 32).

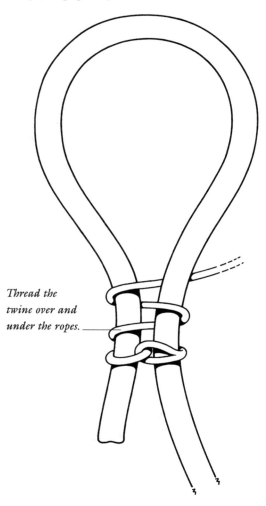

Thread the twine over and under the ropes.

SPLICINGS

Splicing is a method of joining rope to itself or to another rope by interweaving the separate strands. It is a very reliable method and one that every sailor should know.

If you encounter difficulty in separating rope strands, use a fid (see page 17). Most ropework, and especially splicing, benefits from being worked into shape and this can be done by being rolled underfoot or by using a wooden mallet or rubber-faced hammer. All the examples covered in this chapter are illustrated with the most commonly used three-stranded rope.

BACK SPLICE

This is one of the most widely used splices in the sailing world. It is also known as Spanish whipping. It creates a decorative and practical end to a rope and, unlike whipping, it becomes firmer and stronger with time.

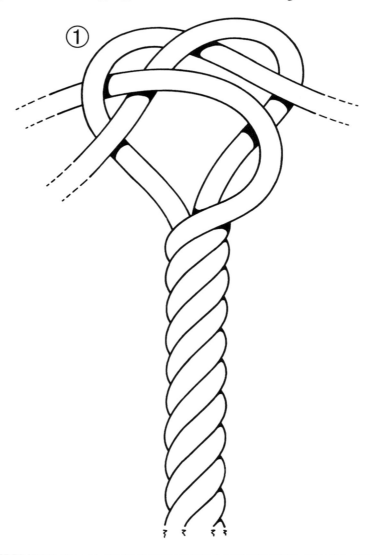

*This splice starts with a crown knot, formed in step
1 and finished in step 2. Pull all the strands tight
to give the appearance of step 2 and then
the splicing can begin.*

The crown knot.

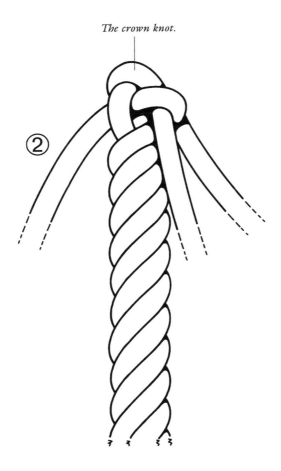

continued on page 38

Back splice

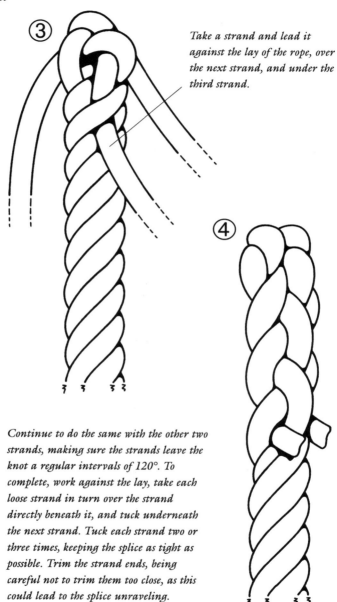

Take a strand and lead it
against the lay of the rope, over
the next strand, and under the
third strand.

Continue to do the same with the other two
strands, making sure the strands leave the
knot a regular intervals of 120°. To
complete, work against the lay, take each
loose strand in turn over the strand
directly beneath it, and tuck underneath
the next strand. Tuck each strand two or
three times, keeping the splice as tight as
possible. Trim the strand ends, being
careful not to trim them too close, as this
could lead to the splice unraveling.

Short Splice

This splice provides the ideal solution for permanently joining the ends of two ropes with little loss of strength. It can also be successfully used to repair a break in a line.

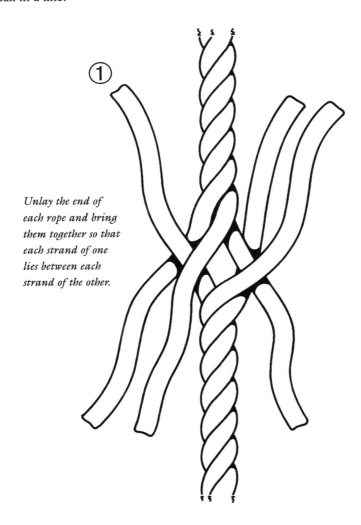

Unlay the end of each rope and bring them together so that each strand of one lies between each strand of the other.

continued on page 40

Short splice

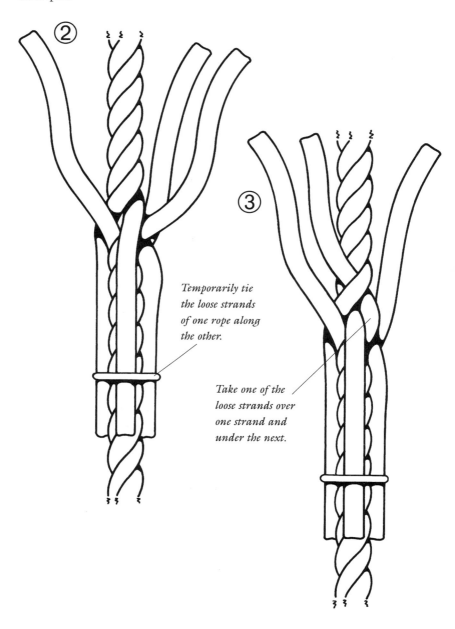

Temporarily tie
the loose strands
of one rope along
the other.

Take one of the
loose strands over
one strand and
under the next.

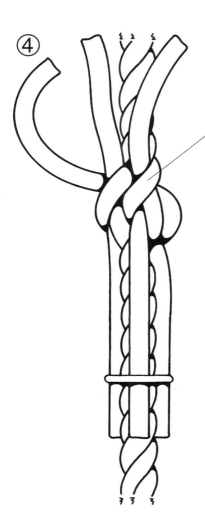

④

Repeat the over-one-under-one tuck with the second and third strand and then repeat the whole process, tucking each strand two or three times.

⑤

To complete, turn the assembly around, remove the temporary fixing, and tuck exactly the same as for the first half. Trim the loose ends, then place the splice on the floor and roll it under your shoe to make it uniformly round.

EYE SPLICE

This is one of the most important sailing knots and one that every sailor should learn. You will always need eyes in the end of your ropes and the eye splice is the most reliable way of achieving this.

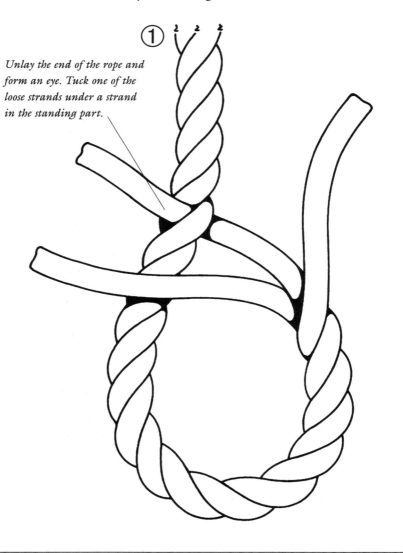

Unlay the end of the rope and form an eye. Tuck one of the loose strands under a strand in the standing part.

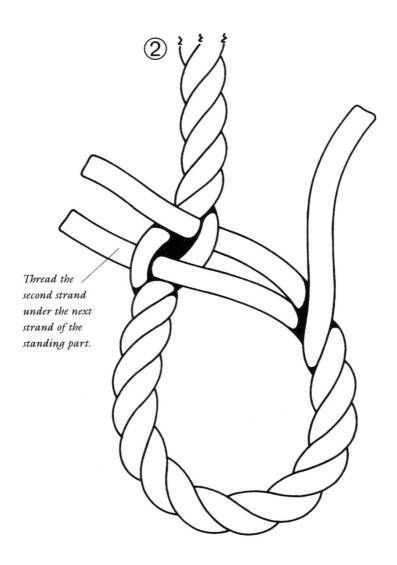

②

Thread the
second strand
under the next
strand of the
standing part.

continued on page 44

Eye splice

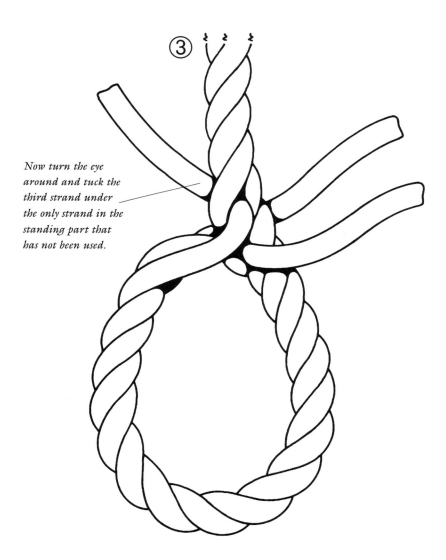

Now turn the eye around and tuck the third strand under the only strand in the standing part that has not been used.

To complete, repeat the process, putting in two more tucks for each strand, making sure the splice is kept as tight as possible. Trim the loose ends and roll the splice between your hands to make it uniformly round.

EYE SPLICE WITH THIMBLE

If subject to heavy use and chafing, an eye splice can be reinforced and strengthened with a thimble. Thimbles are made from various metals or plastic and are available in a wide variety of sizes. The splice can be either tied around or stretched over a thimble.

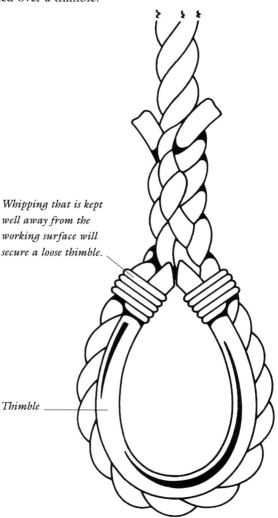

Whipping that is kept well away from the working surface will secure a loose thimble.

Thimble

STOPPER KNOTS

Stopper knots, as their name suggests, are used to prevent the ends of a rope or line slipping through an eye, loop, or hole. They can be used to bind the end of a line so that it will not unravel and can also be used decoratively. At sea they are used to weight lines and at the ends of running rigging.

The most important knot of this type is the overhand. This is the simplest, and perhaps the oldest, knot known to man and is used as a basis for countless others.

OVERHAND KNOT

Also known as the thumb knot, this knot forms the basis for many others. It is used in its own right as a stopper knot and is tied at regular intervals along lines to make them easy to grip. If a line develops an unwanted overhand knot, undo it immediately, as this knot is very difficult to untie, especially when wet.

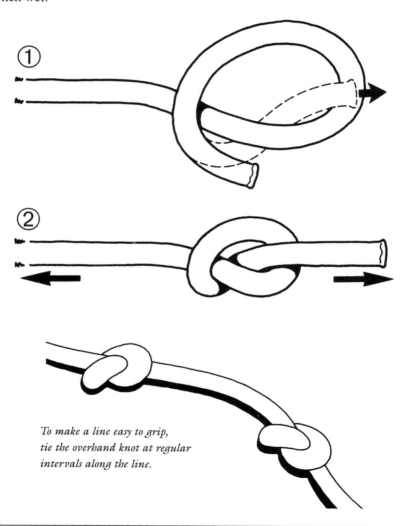

To make a line easy to grip, tie the overhand knot at regular intervals along the line.

Figure-Eight Knot

The knot's name comes from its characteristic shape. It is the most important stopper knot for sailors, used on running rigging. (It is also known as the Flemish knot or Savoy knot).

The knot is made in the end of the line, with the upper loop around the standing part and the lower loop around the working end. When tying this knot you should leave a tail on the working end. This will enable you to grasp the knot should it become jammed.

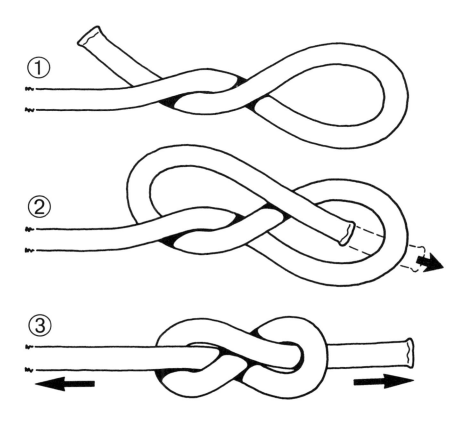

MULTIPLE OVERHAND KNOT

This knot, also known as the blood knot, earned its other name because it was the knot used to weight the ends of the lashes in the cat-o'-nine-tails, the whip used historically to flog soldiers, sailors, and criminals. Its main sailing uses are as a weighting or stopper knot made with small-diameter line.

When tying the knot, keep the loop open and slack as you make the turns and gently pull on both ends at the same time, twisting the two ends in opposite directions. Like many stopper knots, this knot is difficult to untie when the line is wet.

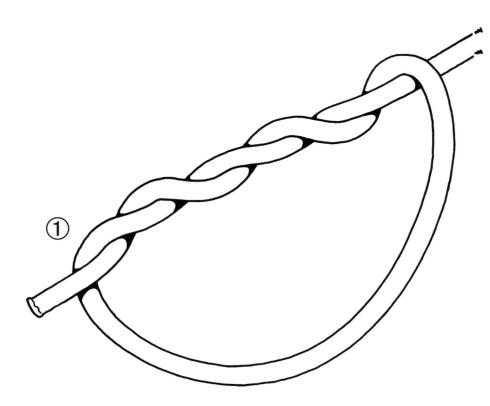

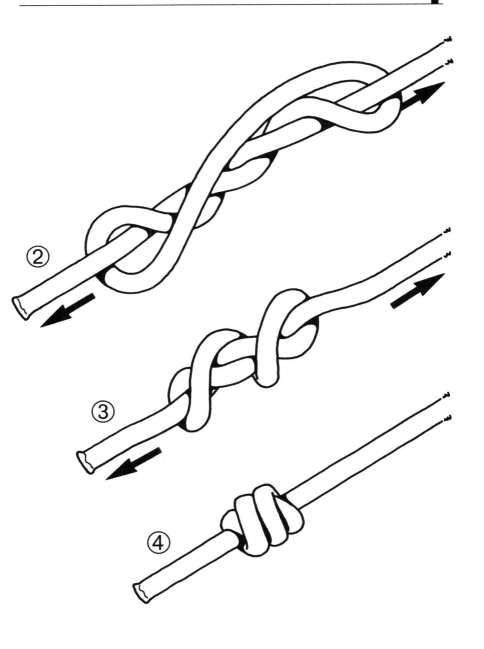

HEAVING LINE KNOT

When a heavy line is thrown from boat to shore or to another vessel, a heaving line knot is used. The heavy line is attached to a *heaving* line, a lighter line that is thrown across the gap first so the heavier line can be drawn behind it. The heaving line knot is tied in the end of this lighter line to give it weight and aid in throwing. Heaving lines are usually one half to three quarters of an inch in diameter and may be up to eighty feet long. They should float, be flexible, and be strong enough to bear a man's weight.

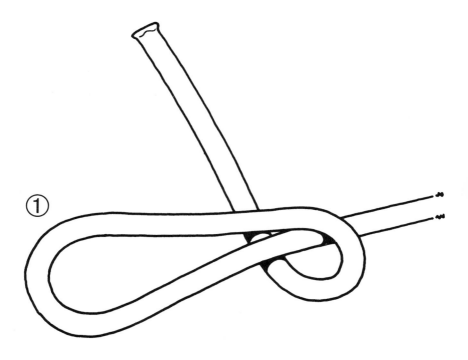

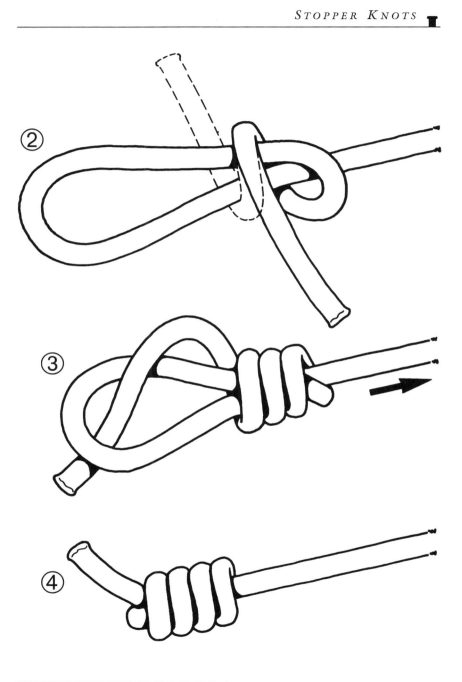

DOUGHNUT

This decorative heaving line knot has the obvious advantage that other lines can be easily tied to it or it can be hooked on or over objects. The weight of this knot can be increased by wrapping a narrow strip of sheet lead around the original three coils before making the final turns. The doughnut also has a very useful secondary use: When it is tied in small material without the sheet lead, it can be used at the end of any cord that you need to pull.

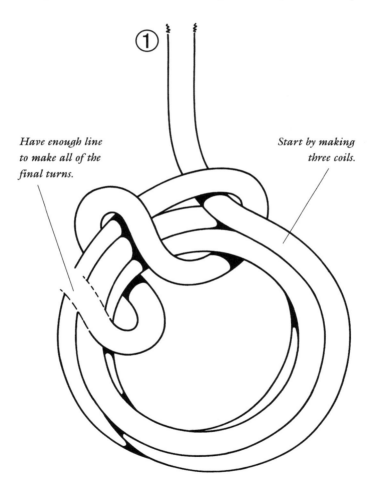

Have enough line to make all of the final turns.

Start by making three coils.

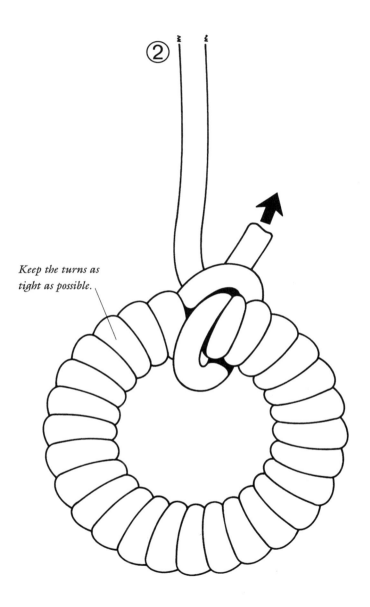

(2)

Keep the turns as
tight as possible.

continued on page 56

Doughnut

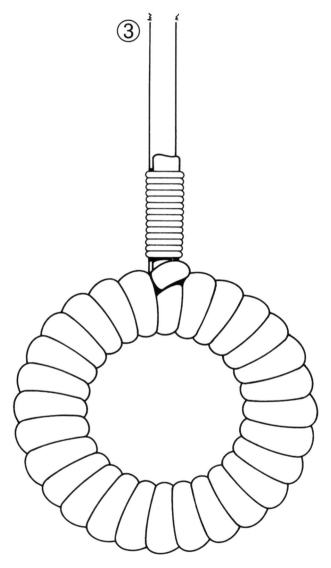

Work the knot into its final circular shape and then trim
and seize the knot end to the standing part.

BENDS

B ends are used to join two lengths of rope at their ends to form one longer piece. It is important, if bends are to be secure, for the ropes joined in this way to be of the same kind and the same diameter. The sheet bend (see page 60) is the exception to this rule. It is secure, even when it is used to join ropes of different diameters.

Bends used at sea can often be made totally secure and more streamlined by seizing any loose ends.

Reef Knot

The reef knot gets its name from its nautical use to tie two ends of a rope when reefing a sail. It is often the only knot many people know, apart from the granny knot.

The reef knot is not a secure bend and should not be used as one, certainly never with ropes of different diameter. Its true function is to join together the ends of the same rope or string. It should *only* be used to make a temporary join in lines of identical type, weight, and diameter where it will not be put under great strain. If the lines have to take strain, stopper knots should be tied in the short ends.

The knot is made up of two half knots. The first half knot starts left over right, the second is added right over left, and both short ends finish on the same side. A correctly tied reef knot is symmetrical. If the knot is raised and uneven, it is a granny knot, which is not secure and should be avoided.

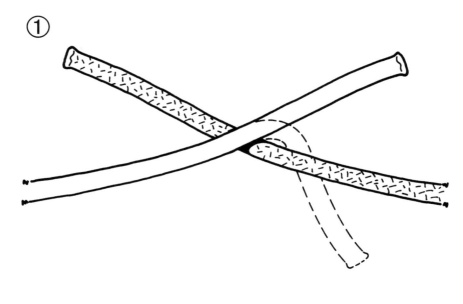

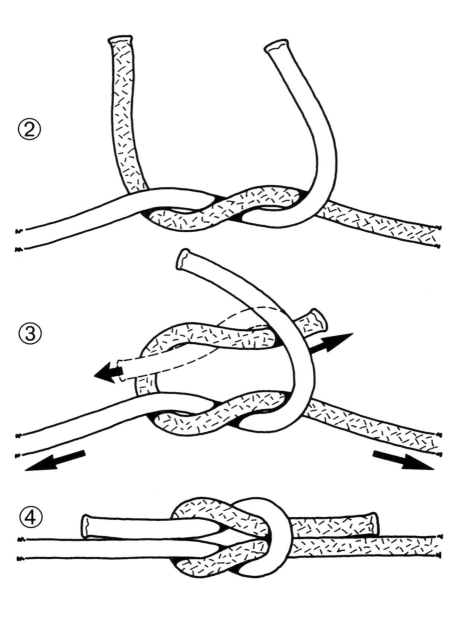

SHEET BEND

The sheet bend is probably the most commonly used of all bends and, unlike most other bends, it can safely join lines of different thickness. It is not, however, 100 percent secure, especially with synthetic rope, and should never be used in circumstances where it will be subjected to great strain. Its breaking strength also decreases in direct proportion to the difference of the lines joined.

The sheet bend derives its name from the way the knot was originally used on sailing ships to secure the ropes (known as sheets) to sails. When put to its other traditional use, as the knot used to join the corners of a flag to the rope when it is hoisted and lowered, it is known as the flag bend. It is quick to make and easy to untie, by rolling forward the bight encircling the single line, and is one of the basic knots that all sailors should know.

A slipped sheet bend is formed by placing a bight between the loop of the heavier rope and the standing part of the lighter one. The slipped knot is easiest to untie when the rope is under strain.

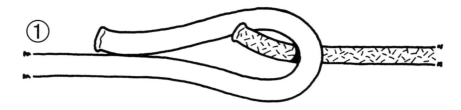

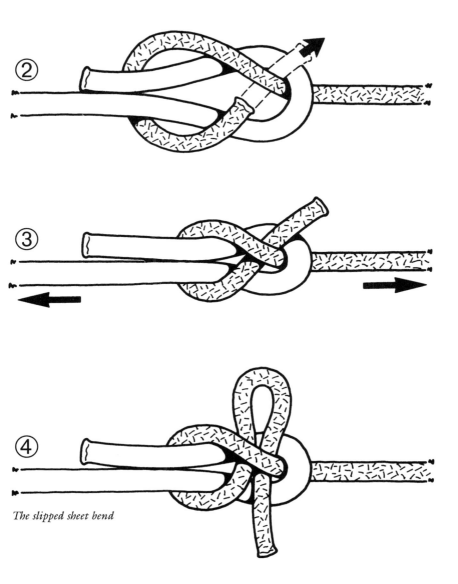

② ③ ④

The slipped sheet bend

CARRICK BEND

Its name probably derives from a medieval Western European ship, the carrack. The knot is formed from two overhand knots crossing each other. It is a very stable knot, does not slip, and is one of the most secure ways of joining two ropes of similar diameter but different type. It is rarely used as a temporary knot as it is very hard to undo when wet or if it has been subjected to very heavy strain. It can be used with larger-diameter ropes such as hawsers, tow lines, and warp ropes.

In its flat form it is valued for its distinctive symmetric appearance and has long been a favorite among artists and graphic designers. When it is drawn up it capsizes into an entirely different shape, but this has no detrimental effect on its strength or security.

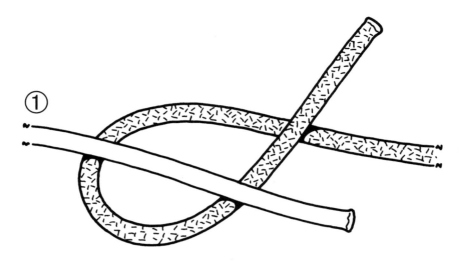

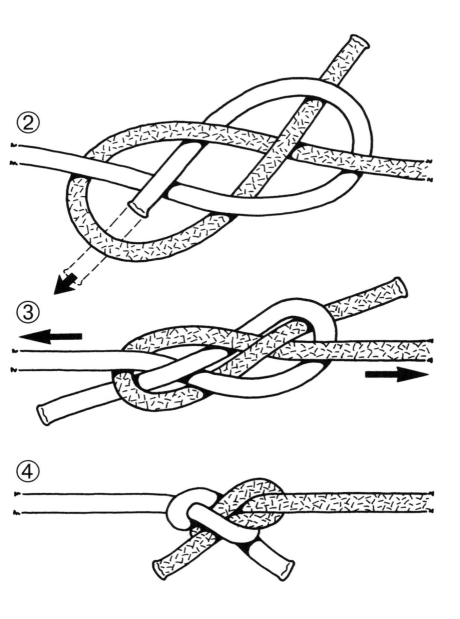

RIGGER'S BEND

The rigger's bend or Hunter's bend is based on two overhand knots. It is stable, has good grip, and is stronger than the sheet bend or the reef knot. It also has the advantage of being easy to untie.

The name Hunter's bend came from Dr. Edward Hunter, a retired physician, who was reported to have invented the knot in 1968. Subsequent research, however, revealed his knot to be the same as the rigger's bend described nearly twenty years earlier by Phil D. Smith in an American book called *Knots for Mountaineers*. He had devised the knot while working on the waterfront in San Francisco. Whoever first invented it, the rigger's bend or the Hunter's bend remains a good general-purpose sailing knot with many useful qualities.

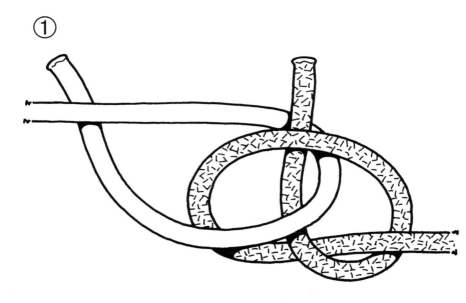

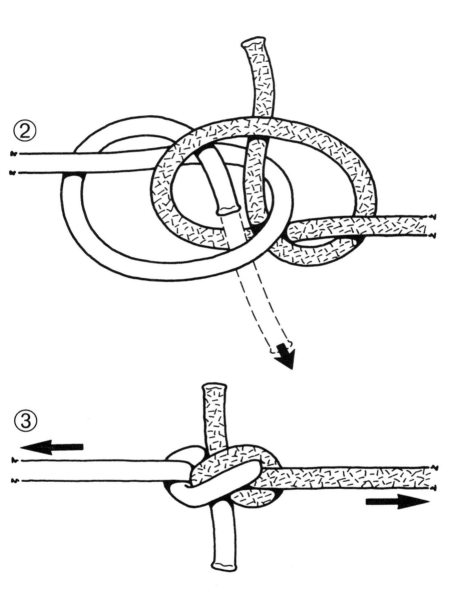

SURGEON'S KNOT

This knot, as the name suggests, is used by surgeons to suture wounds and tie off blood vessels. It is also an excellent sailing knot for joining two lengths of rope or line together. It is less bulky than other knots and has a good grip. It twists as it is drawn up tight and the diagonal is wrapped around it.

①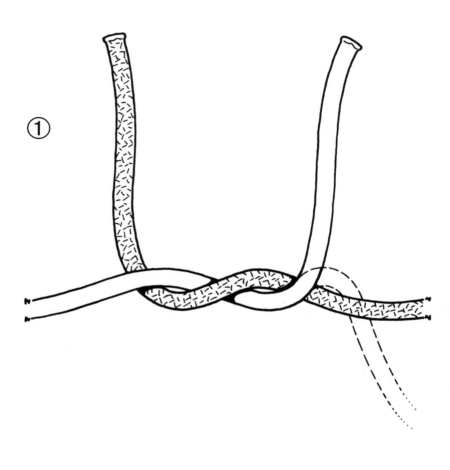

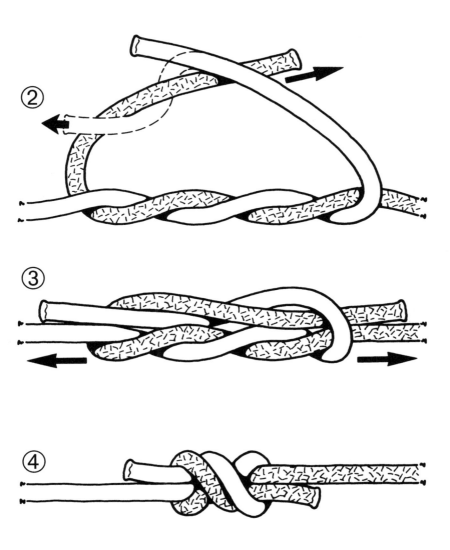

FISHERMAN'S KNOT

This knot is said to have been invented in the nineteenth century, but some authorities suggest it was known to the ancient Greeks. It is generally known as the fisherman's knot, but over the years it has picked up many different names (such as angler's knot, English knot, Englishman's bend, halibut knot, true lover's knot, and waterman's knot). It is formed from two overhand knots that jam against each other; the short ends are on opposite sides and lie almost parallel to their nearest standing part. After use, the two component knots are generally easily separated and undone.

The fisherman's knot is best suited to joining thin lines such as string, cord, twine, or small stuff, and as the name suggests, it is widely used by fishermen for joining the finest of fishing lines.

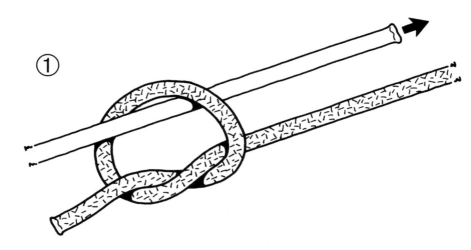

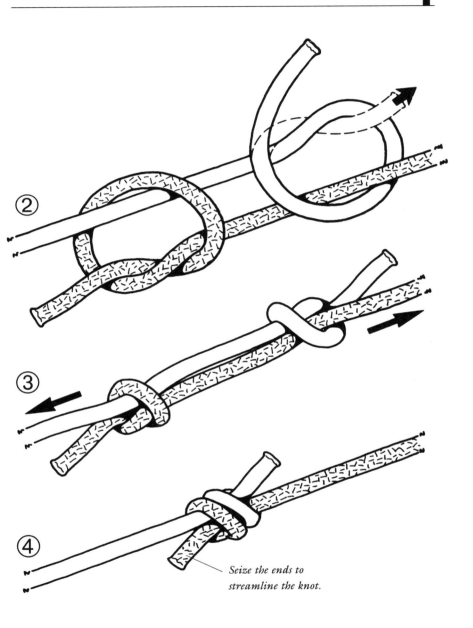

② ③ ④

Seize the ends to
streamline the knot.

DOUBLE FISHERMAN'S KNOT

This double version of the fisherman's knot is a very strong knot for joining thin lines. It is also known as the grapevine knot. It is quite a bulky knot, so often the ends are seized to streamline the knot and prevent it from catching.

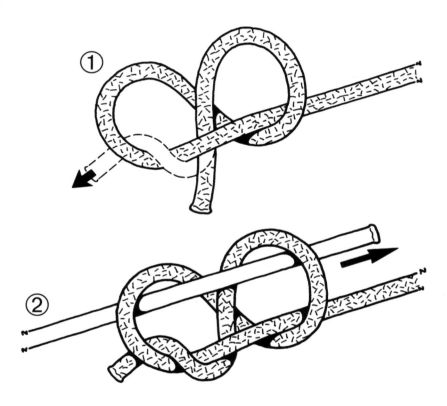

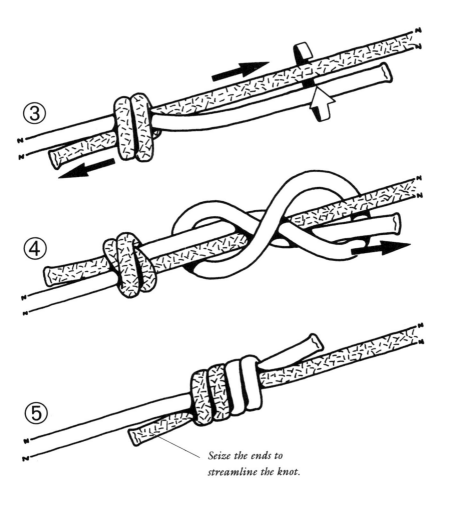

③

④

⑤

Seize the ends to
streamline the knot.

Figure-Eight Bend

This simple knot (also known as the Flemish bend or knot) is tied by making a figure-eight knot in one end of a line and then following it around with the other working end. It is, despite its simplicity, one of the strongest bends and holds equally well in string and rope.

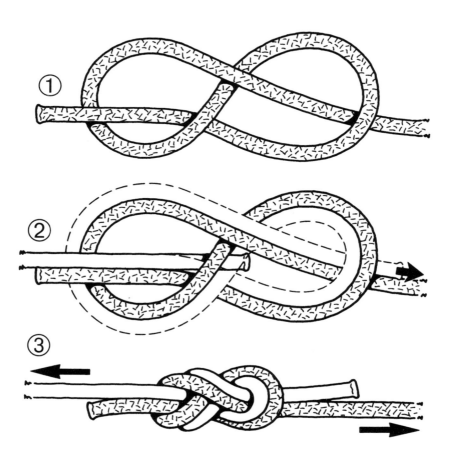

LOOPS

Knots made in the end of rope by folding it back into an eye or loop and then knotting it to its own standing part are called loops. Unlike hitches, which are formed around an object and follow its shape, loops are made in the hand, generally to drop over an object.

Loops are the most commonly used group of sailing knots, and are particularly important to sailors.

FIGURE-EIGHT LOOP

This knot is relatively easy to tie and stays tied, even when stiff rope is used. It has many sailing applications, especially when a quick, but strong, eye or loop is required at the end of a rope. Its disadvantages—it is difficult to adjust and cannot easily be untied after loading—tend to be outweighed by its usefulness. It is also known as the figure-eight on the bight.

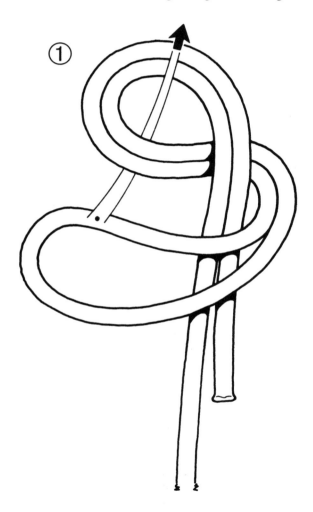

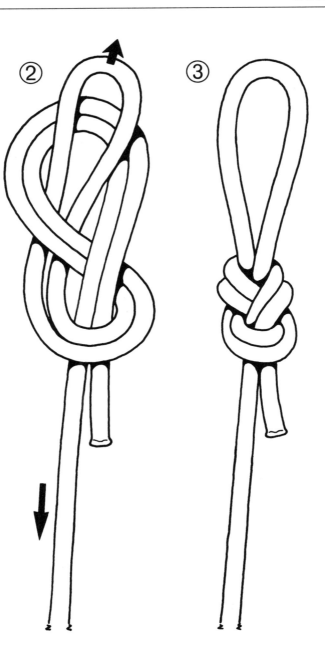

BOWLINE

The bowline is one of the best known and widely used knots and is particularly important to sailors. It is tied to form a fixed loop at the end of a line or to attach a rope to an object. It has many sailing applications, including use on running rigging and for hoisting, joining, and salvage work.

The bowline is simple to tie, strong, and stable. Its main advantages are that it does not slip or come loose, even in polypropylene ropes that allow other knots to slip. It is also quick and easy to untie, even when the line is under tension, by pushing forward the bight that encircles the standing part of the line.

For extra security, finish the bowline off with a stopper knot or an extra half hitch.

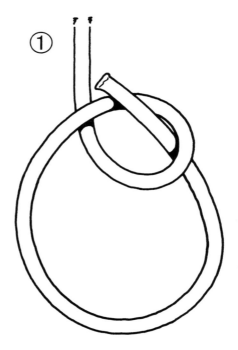

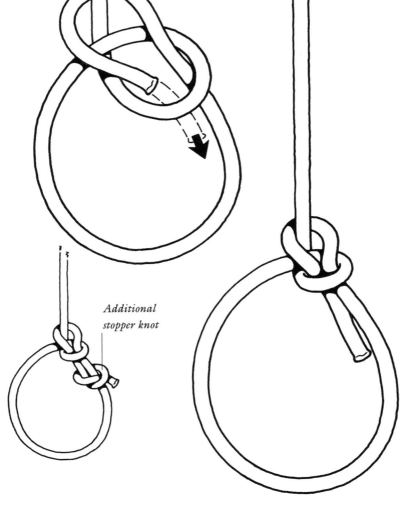

② ③

Additional stopper knot

RUNNING BOWLINE

This is probably the only running knot used by sailors; it is used on running rigging and to retrieve floating objects that have fallen overboard. On the old sailing ships this knot was used in high winds to tighten the square sail to the yardarm.

The running bowline has many uses because it is strong and secure, does not weaken rope, is simple to untie, and slides easily. It is useful for hanging objects with ropes of unequal diameters—the weight of the object creates the tension that makes the knot grip.

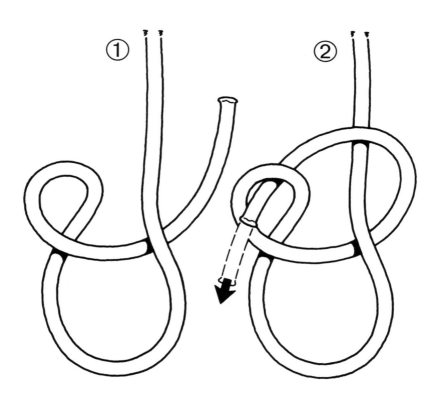

③ ④

BOWLINE ON A BIGHT

The bowline on a bight forms two fixed loops that do not slide. They are of the same diameter and overlap each other but, when opened out, they can be used separately. Although an ancient knot, it is still used today—especially in sea rescues. If the person to be rescued is conscious, he or she puts a leg through each loop and holds on to the standing part. If the person is unconscious, both legs are put through one loop and the other loop goes under the armpits. This knot is equally effective in salvaging objects.

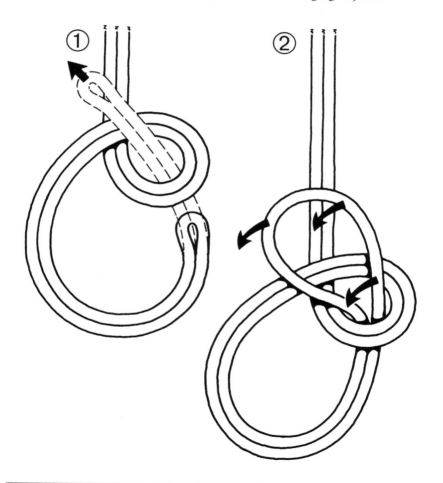

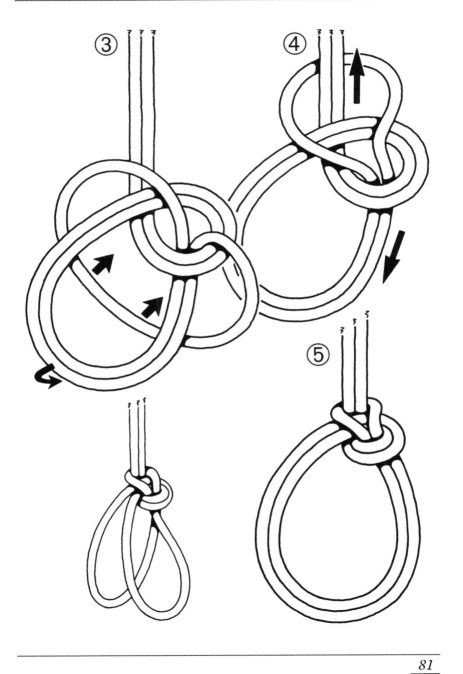

Bowline – Rope Under Tension

This variation for tying the bowline is particularly useful for attaching boats to rings. The standing part stays taut throughout while the working end is used to tie a secure fastening.

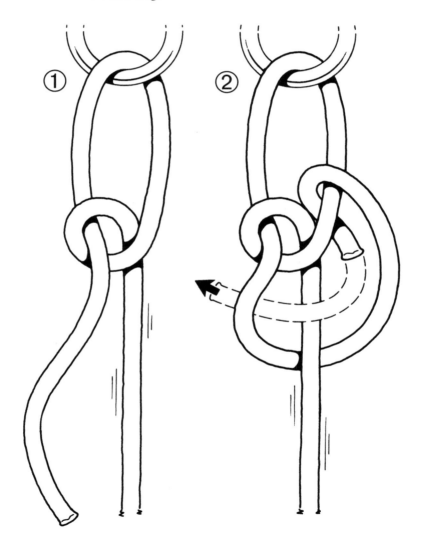

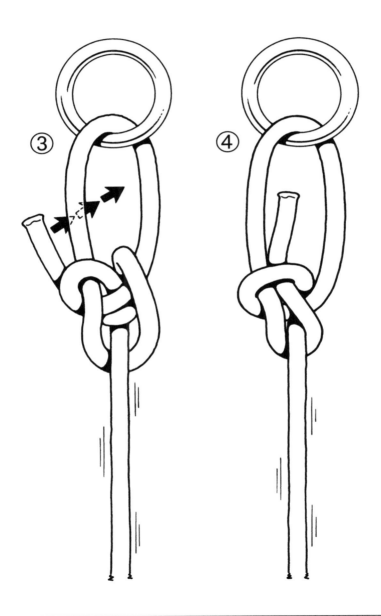

③

④

THREE-PART CROWN

This sturdy, secure, double loop knot can be used as a decorative knot from which to hang gear or equipment, aboard ship or on shore.

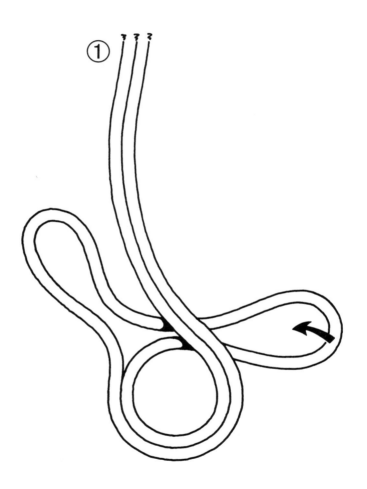

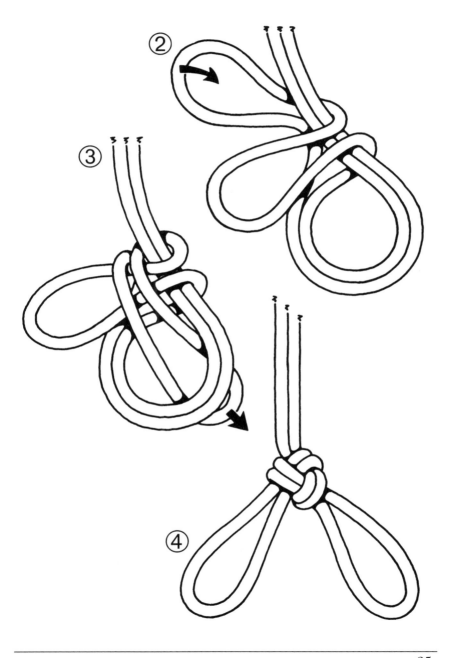

SPANISH BOWLINE

This is a very strong knot that is widely used in rescue work at sea. The Spanish bowline can also be used to hoist large objects in a horizontal position.

Like the bowline on a bight (see page 80), it is a very old knot, formed of two separate and independent loops that will hold securely and are very safe, even under considerable strain. To effect a rescue, one loop is slipped over the casualty's head, around the back and under the armpits; the other loop goes around the legs behind the knees. It is vitally important that each loop is tightened to the individual's size and then locked into position. If this is not done properly, an unconscious casualty could easily fall through the loops.

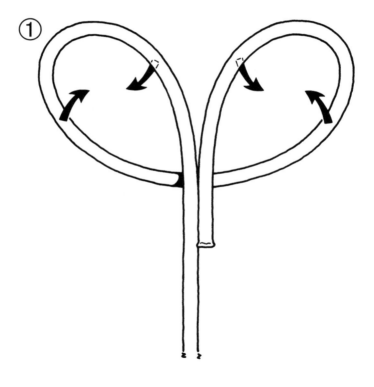

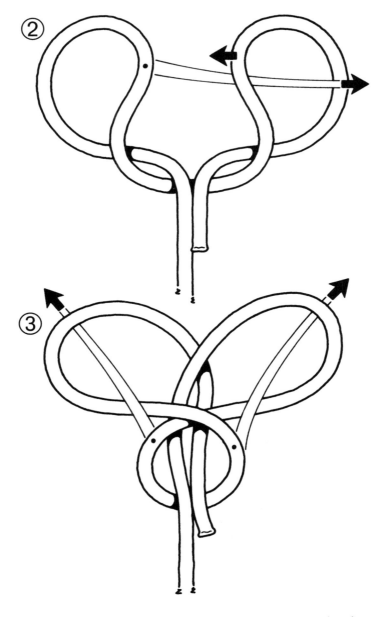

continued on page 88

Spanish bowline

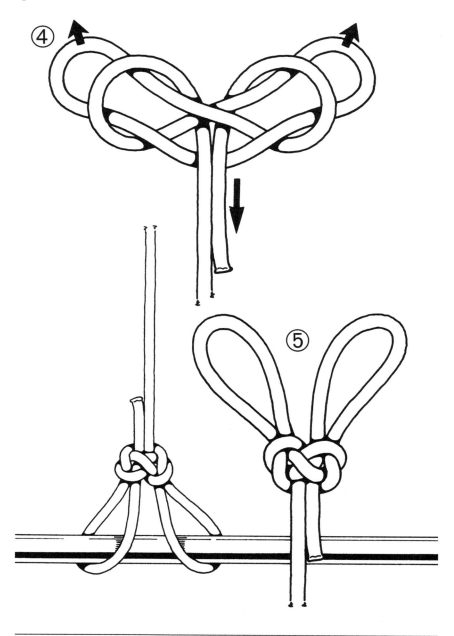

HITCHES

Hitches are knots used to secure a rope to another object (such as a post, hook, spar, rail), or another rope that does not play any part in the actual tying.

They are widely used in sailing for mooring boats, fastening lines, and lashing. They can stand parallel strain without slipping and have the advantage of once learned, being very quick to tie.

HALF HITCHES

The half hitch is a very widely used fastening. It is, in fact, a single hitch formed around the standing part of another hitch. It is used to complete and strengthen other knots—as in the round turn and two half hitches—which can then be used for tying, hanging, hooking objects, etc. The slipped half hitch is a useful variation of the simple half hitch; a sharp pull on the end releases the knot.

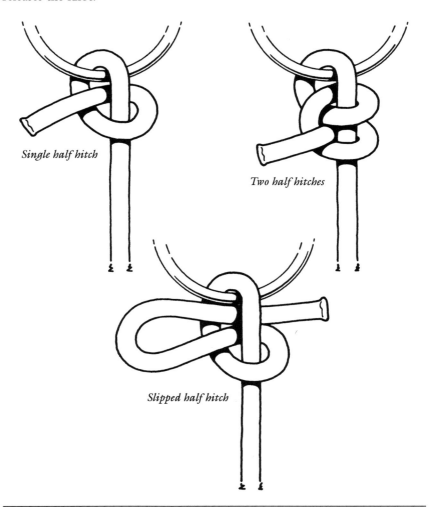

Single half hitch

Two half hitches

Slipped half hitch

CLOVE HITCH

The clove hitch is one of the best known and most valuable of hitches and is used extensively on most yachts. It can be used to fasten a line to a rail, post, or bollard, or on to another rope that is not part of the knot. It can, with practice, be tied with one hand. As one of its other names, the boatman's knot, suggests, it is particularly useful for sailors who may need to moor a dinghy to a dock with one hand while holding on to a rail with the other.

The clove hitch is not, however, a totally secure mooring knot, as it will work loose if the strain is intermittent and comes from different angles. It is best used as a temporary hold, and then replaced by a more stable knot. It can be made more secure by making one or two half hitches around the standing part of the rope, or by adding a stopper knot.

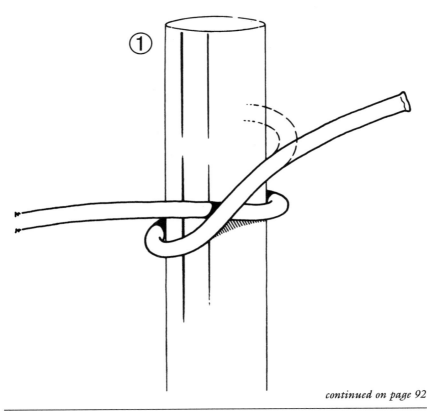

continued on page 92

Clove hitch

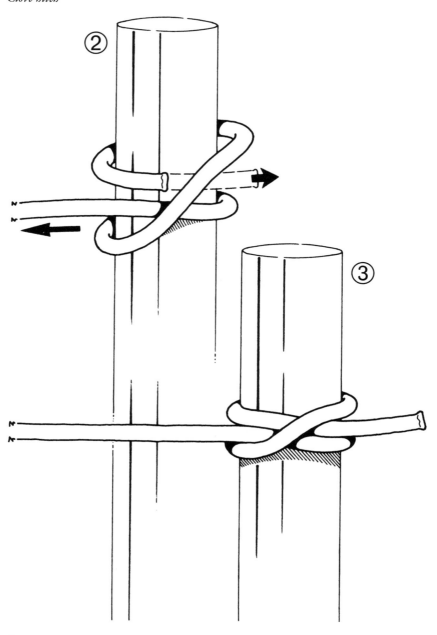

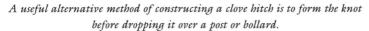
A useful alternative method of constructing a clove hitch is to form the knot before dropping it over a post or bollard.

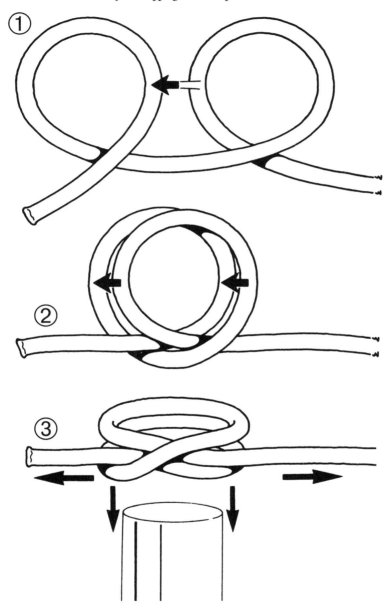

CONSTRICTOR KNOT

This is a popular all-purpose knot because it is firm and does not slip. It is particularly useful for creating a quick temporary whipping on the ends of ropes.

The knot is made by taking two turns with the rope, forming an overhand knot in the second. The left end is then threaded under the first turn, trapping the overhand knot under a crosswise turn that holds it firmly in place. The constrictor knot grips firmly and stays tied. It may have to be cut free unless the last tuck is made with a bight to make a slip knot.

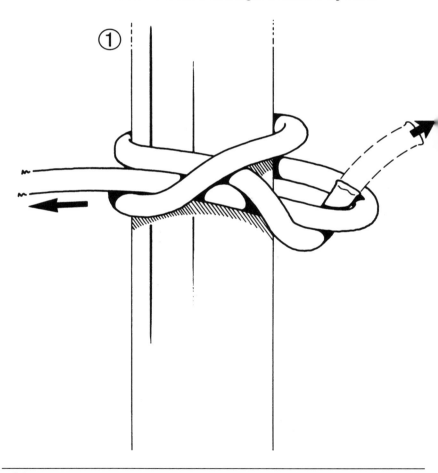

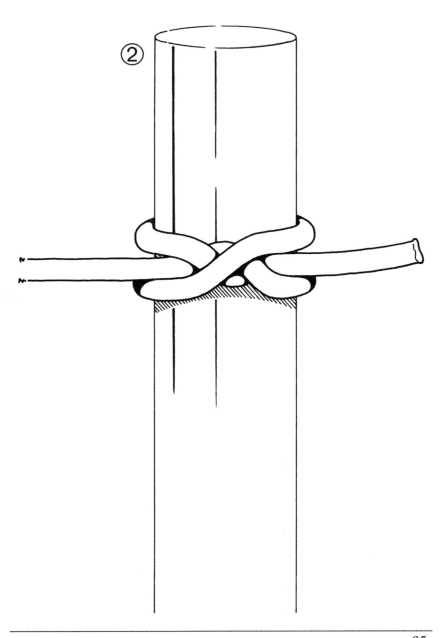

Transom Knot

This is similar to a constrictor knot (see page 94). It is used to fix together crossed pieces of rigid material and has a wide range of sailing uses; for example, to secure paddles to luggage racks. If used as a permanent knot, the ends may be trimmed off for neatness.

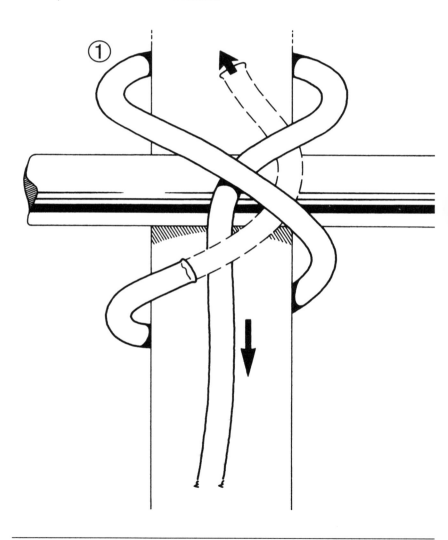

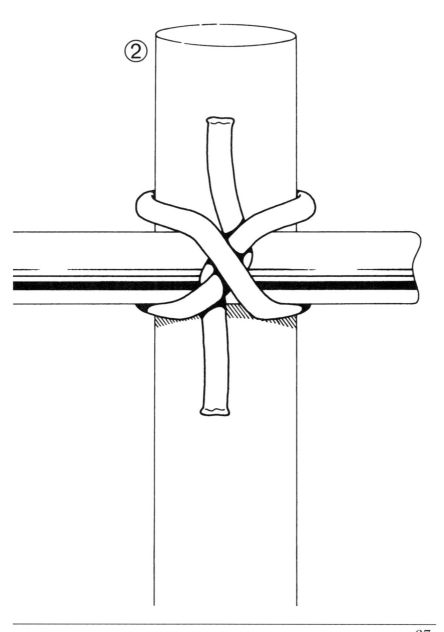

PILE HITCH

The pile hitch is a very neat and practical hitch for securing objects to a post. It is ideal for a temporary mooring of a boat. The big advantage of this hitch is that it is very easy to tie quickly.

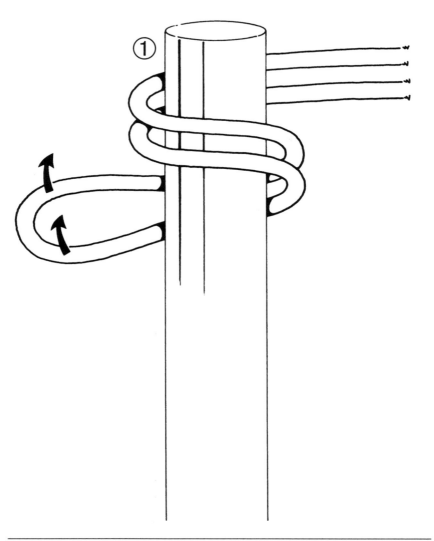

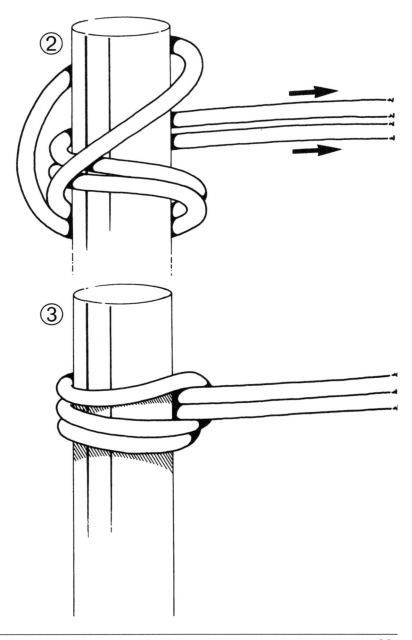

Round Turn and Two Half Hitches

This knot is strong, dependable, and never jams. This makes it a very versatile sailing knot; you can use it whenever you want to fasten a line to a ring, post, bollard, deck eye, rail, or beam. It moors boats safely and will support heavy loads. It has another advantage in that once one end has been secured with a round turn and two half hitches, the other end can be tied with a second knot. This is especially useful when fastening unwieldy, bulky objects.

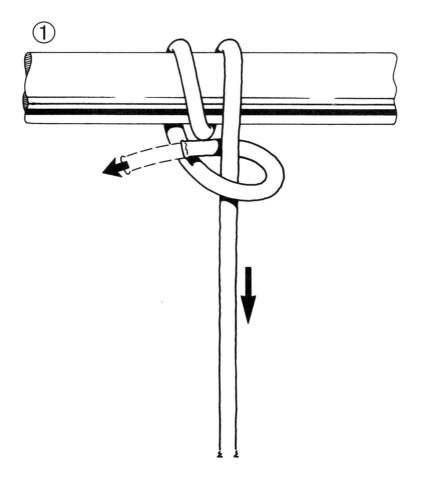

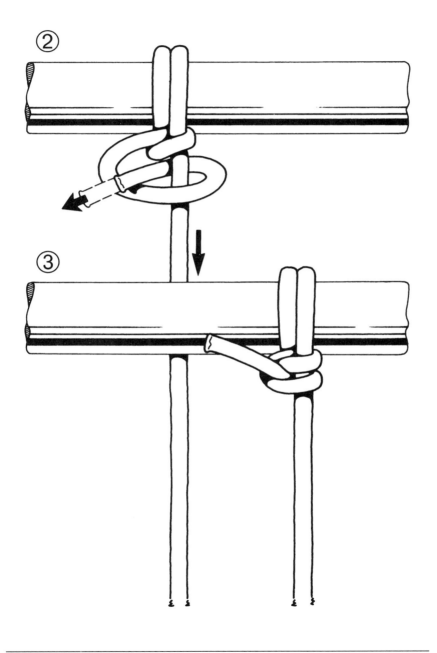

ANCHOR BEND

The anchor bend, also known a the fisherman's bend, is one of the most secure and widely used sailing hitches. It is formed by making two turns around a post or through a ring and then tucking the working end through both turns.

An additional stopper knot or half hitch can be used for added safety, but if the anchor bend is to be used as a long-term fixing (for example, to tie onto an anchor ring), the working end should be secured with a seizing for total security.

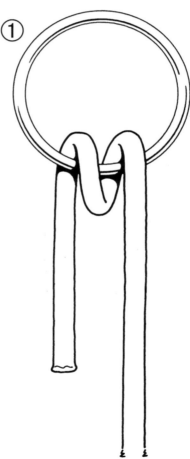

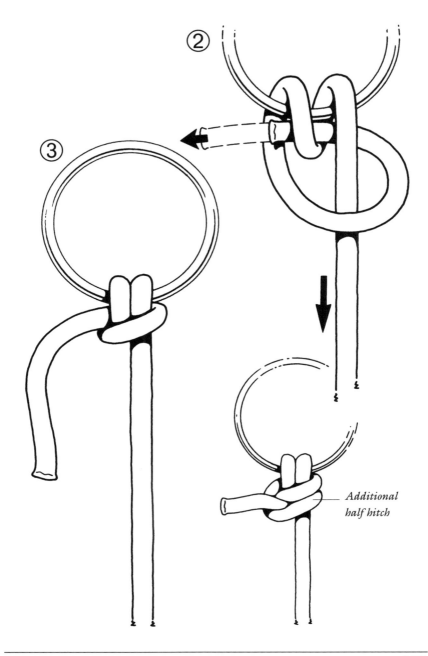

②

③

*Additional
half hitch*

Buntline Hitch

This hitch is specifically used for attaching buntlines to to the eyes or eyelet holes on sails. The buntline hitch needs to be very secure so as to avoid loosening in strong winds that constantly buffet sails. Its strength comes from the short end being deliberately trapped inside the knot.

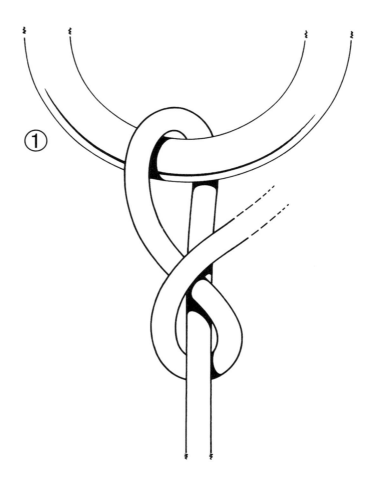

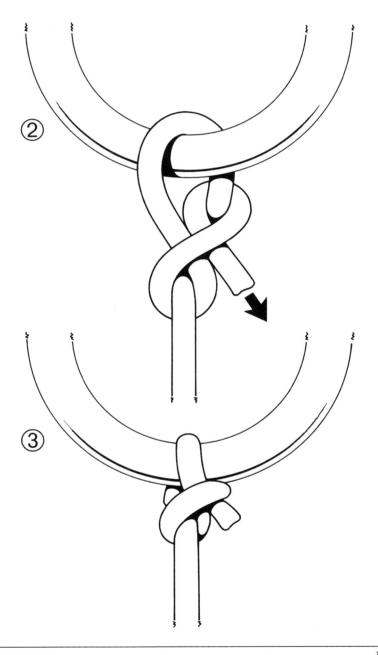

ROLLING HITCH

This is an essential knot for sailboarders. It is derived from the clove hitch but is significantly more secure. It is used on sailboards to secure the wishbone boom to the mast, but can equally well be used to make any line fast to other cylindrical objects. This very effective, reliable knot is easy to tie and it grips itself, but only in one direction.

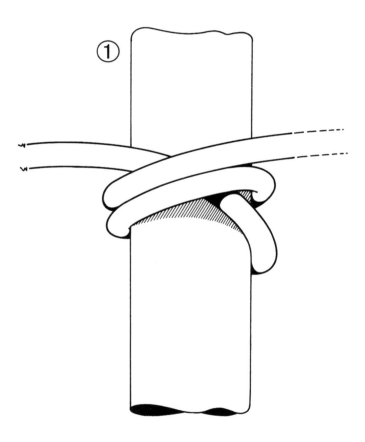

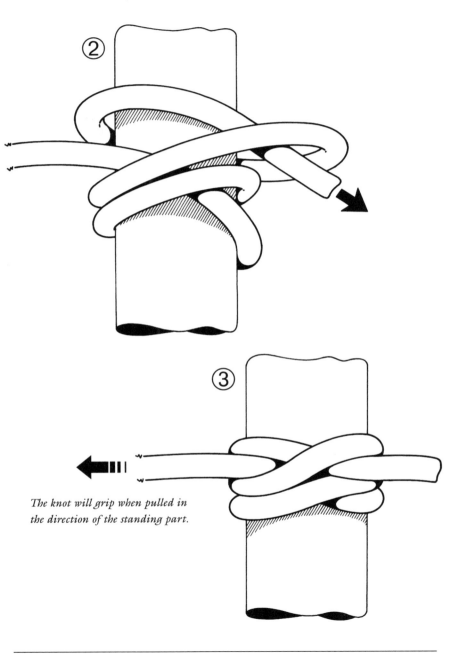

② ③

*The knot will grip when pulled in
the direction of the standing part.*

WAGGONER'S HITCH

The waggoner's hitch is a very useful, practical knot that makes it possible to pull tight a line or rope yet leave it ready for immediate release. This makes it an ideal knot for securing loads or deck gear. Once the line has been heaved tight, it should be secured with at least two half hitches.

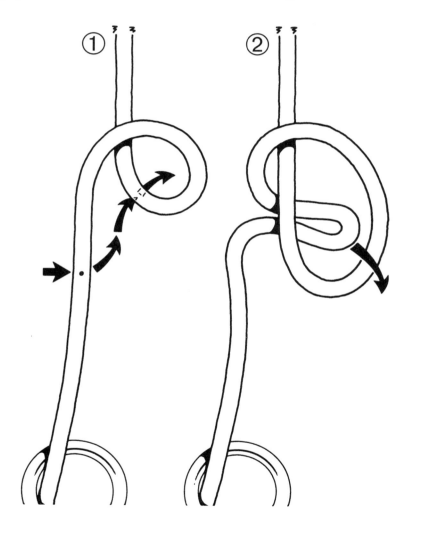

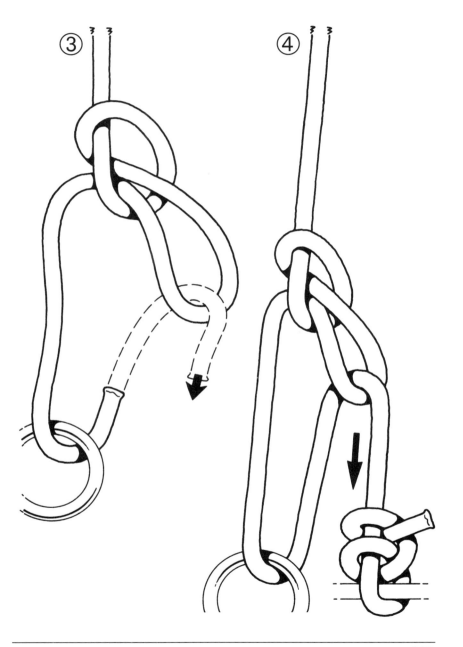

CAT'S PAW

This is the best hook knot for rope of medium diameter because the strain is equal on both sides. It has a long history of use on the docks and at sea for lifting and slinging heavy loads. This very secure knot can be used, for example, on the hook of a crane in the marina.

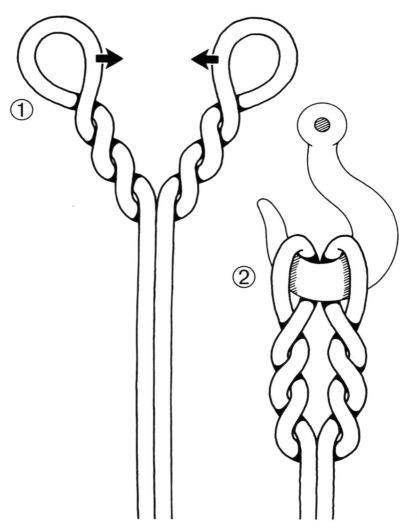

DECORATIVE
KNOTS

Decorative knots can be used individually or in elaborate combinations; they can be used for pure decoration or in the case of sailing for some very practical purposes.

Many decorative knots have long nautical traditions, and seamen and sailors, particularly those who served aboard the great sailing vessels of the eighteenth and nineteen centuries, made decorative knot tying into a branch of folk art.

Knife Lanyard Knot

A lanyard is usually worn around the the neck or attached to a belt for the purpose of holding a wide variety of objects—from knives and whistles to watches and binoculars. Lanyards have a long nautical tradition and because the cord is left in view, sailors often decorated them with a range of elaborate knots. The knife lanyard knot is one of the most attractive and subsequently one of the most widely used. At first sight it may appear difficult to tie, but be patient, follow the step-by-step instructions, "work" the knot into its final form, and you will be rewarded with a beautiful and functional decorative knot.

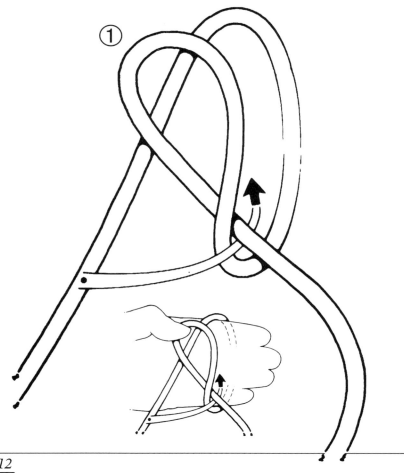

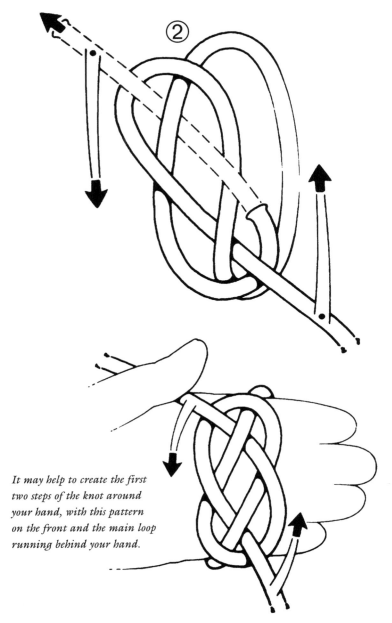

②

It may help to create the first
two steps of the knot around
your hand, with this pattern
on the front and the main loop
running behind your hand.

continued on page 114

Knife lanyard knot

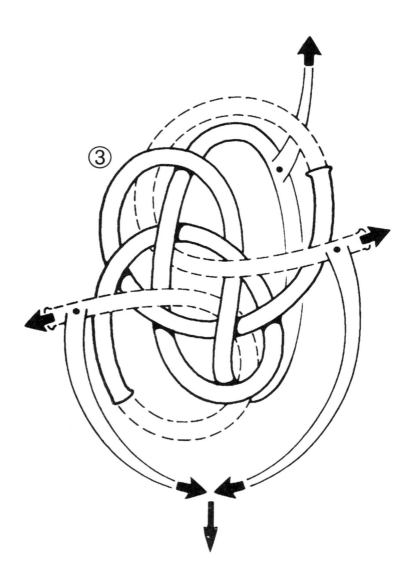

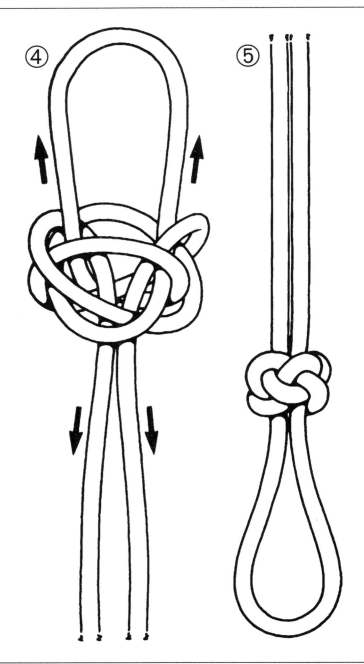

Flat Sinnet

Sinnets are one or more intertwined strands that can be tied from a wide variety of materials. They have a vast range of decorative applications, but also have many practical advantages. In the past sailors exploited the excellent "cling" and surface wear qualities of "sinnet lines."

This simple, three-strand, plait or braid sinnet is also know as the English or common sinnet. Arrange the three strands as in step 1 and if necessary secure them in a straight line with a clip or clamp. To achieve a neat, compact sinnet as in step 6, tighten and arrange the plait at each step of the tying. Sinnets can be finished off in a variety of ways, depending on their final use. The simplest method is by clamping or seizing with thin string and then trimming off the excess.

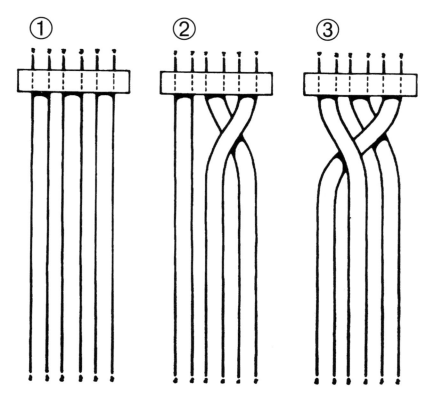

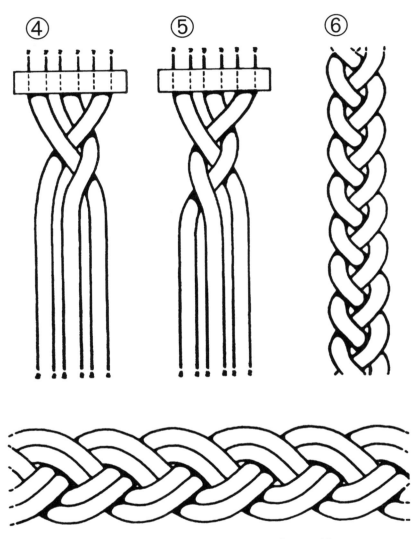

This attractive variation of the flat sinnet is created by doubling the strands. Use six strands, arranged in three pairs, and follow exactly the same tying procedure.

Monkey's Fist

The monkey's fist is a decorative knot that also has many practical uses, the most common being the knot at the end of a heaving line. To give the monkey's fist more weight, it is often tied over a spherical object such as a heavy ball or stone. Smaller knots can be tied over golf balls and if the line is required to float, use a rubber ball. Decoratively, it makes an attractive end to any cord, and is regularly used at the end of pull cords.

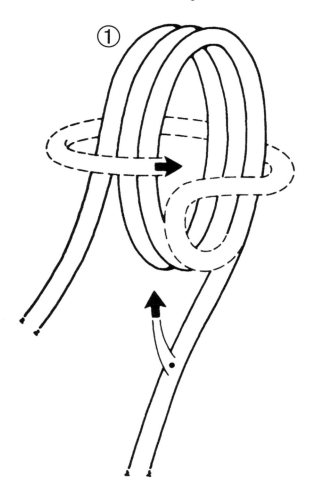

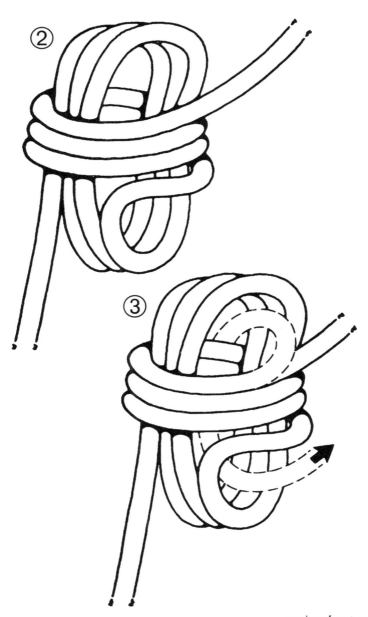

continued on page 120

Monkey's fist

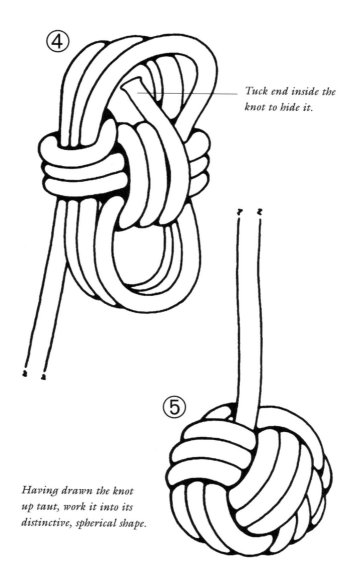

④

Tuck end inside the knot to hide it.

⑤

Having drawn the knot up taut, work it into its distinctive, spherical shape.

*This alternative way of tying a monkey's fist
brings both ends out of the knot.*

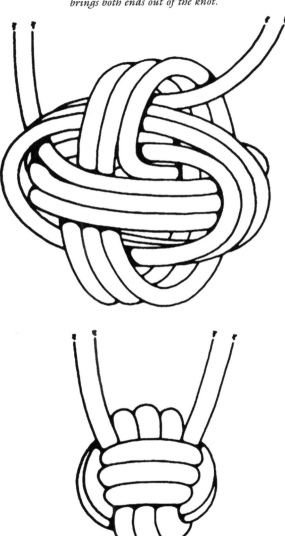

TURK'S HEAD

Turk's head knots have long been recognized for their highly decorative attributes. Leonardo da Vinci drew them in the fifteenth century and they are still widely used today. They are usually tied around cylindrical objects—in most cases as pure decoration (for example, to decorate a tiller). But they can also serve many practical sailing purposes, and are often used to mark the position of center rudder on the ship's wheel.

There are many recorded variations of these knots. The Turk's head shown here, a single-strand, four-lead, three-bight version, is one of the most popular. To create the finished compact knot as in step 6, the slack will need to be worked out. This is done gradually, by starting at one end of the cord and progressing right through the knot to the other end. It may also help to use a pair of thin-nosed pliers.

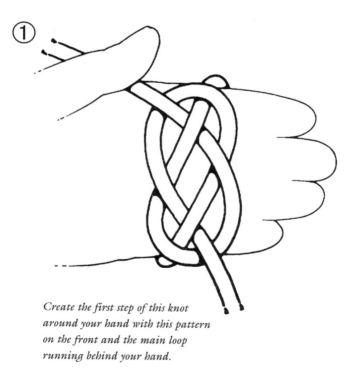

Create the first step of this knot around your hand with this pattern on the front and the main loop running behind your hand.

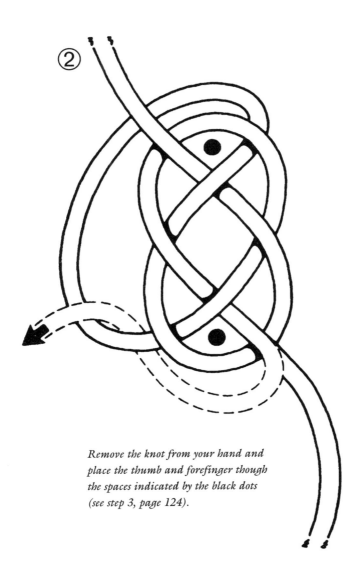

Remove the knot from your hand and place the thumb and forefinger though the spaces indicated by the black dots (see step 3, page 124).

continued on page 124

Turk's head

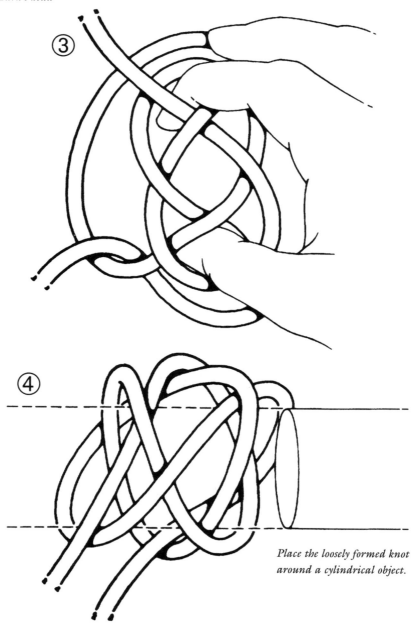

③

④

Place the loosely formed knot around a cylindrical object.

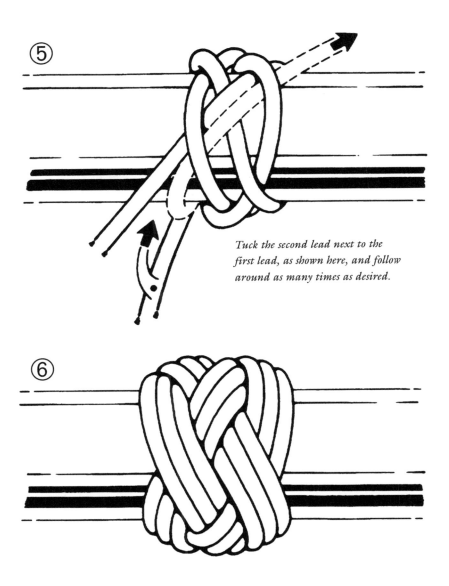

⑤

Tuck the second lead next to the first lead, as shown here, and follow around as many times as desired.

⑥

Turk's Head – Flat Form

This method shows how to tie a Turk's head in a flat form. The knot can be left in this form to create, for example, a mat or decorative fender. Alternatively, it can be turned down and worked over a cylindrical object to form a decorative covering.

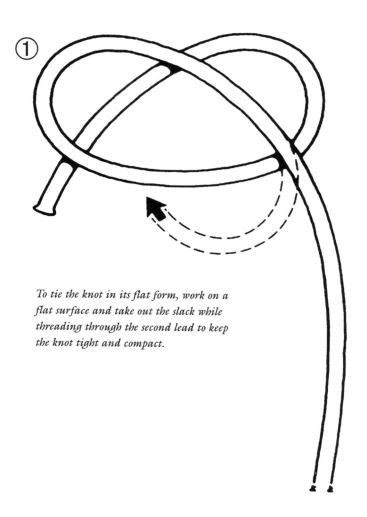

To tie the knot in its flat form, work on a flat surface and take out the slack while threading through the second lead to keep the knot tight and compact.

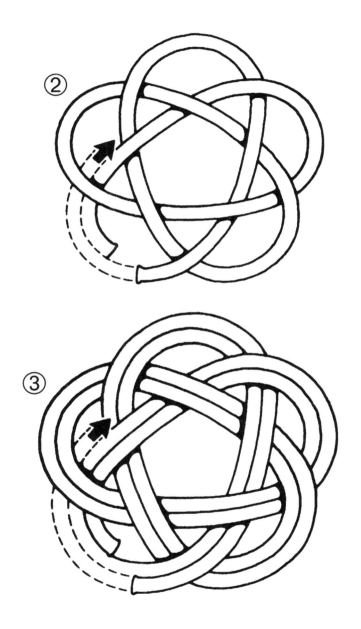

continued on page 128

Turk's head – flat form

The first lead can be followed around by the second lead
as many times as required to create the finished knot.
Always keep the second lead on the same side as the first
lead (the lead that created the pattern) and tuck
the ends in neatly to hide them.

OCEAN PLAT

This classic flat knot is found all over the world in a surprising number of situations but its use as a mat or tread aboard ship or boat is one of the common and practical uses.

The size of the example shown here, which is one of the most widely used, is based on three side bights. The pattern can be made more solid by increasing the number of times the lead is followed around, but the actual size of the knot cannot be increased. To increase the size of the knot, the number of bights has to be increased. For example, increase to six or nine bights to create a long, narrow ocean plat for a companionway aboard ship or boat.

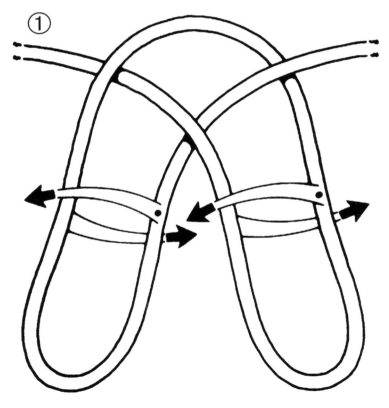

continued on page 130

Ocean plat

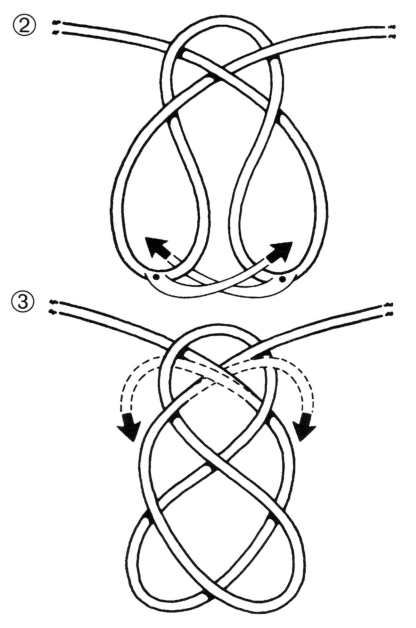

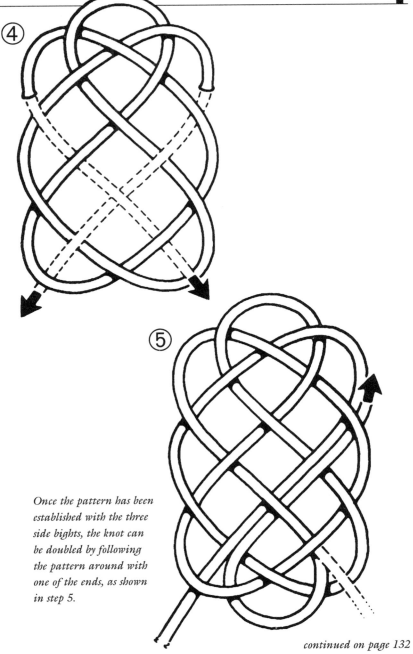

Once the pattern has been established with the three side bights, the knot can be doubled by following the pattern around with one of the ends, as shown in step 5.

continued on page 132

Ocean plat

The knot can be doubled or followed around as
many times as desired. It can also be left loosely
formed as shown above, or it can be tightened
and made solid, as in step 7.

To finish, hide the ends by tucking them into the weave on the
underside of the knot. If the knot is to be used as a mat, the
whole structure can be greatly stengthened by sewing together
all of the intersecting points with strong thread.

NET MAKING

Nets can be tied in a variety of sizes for many different uses, from fishing to storage, and it is always useful to be able to construct your own custom-sized net. One of the most popular, and important, sailing uses is safety netting between guardrails and deck. This does not only prevent people, especially small children, from falling overboard, but it also prevents the loss of important equipment that can often prove impossible to recover.

To construct a net you will require a reel of good netting twine, a net needle, and a piece of wood with straight edges.

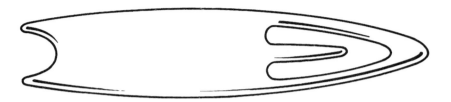

*A net needle will make it easy to thread the twine
and save you from having to pull the whole line
through at each turn.*

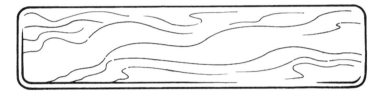

*A wooden straightedge will enable you to
hold and check the mesh to give a
uniform pattern.*

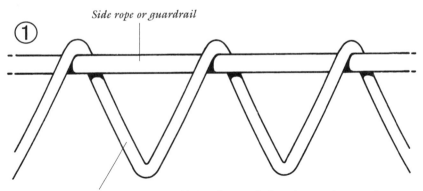

Side rope or guardrail

①

*Looped netting twine. For additional strength the twine can be secured
to the side rope or guardrail by using a clove hitch at each apex.*

continued on page 136

Net making

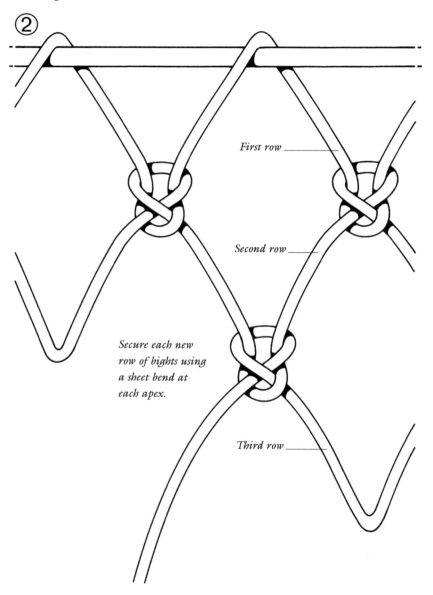

② First row

Second row

Secure each new
row of bights using
a sheet bend at
each apex.

Third row

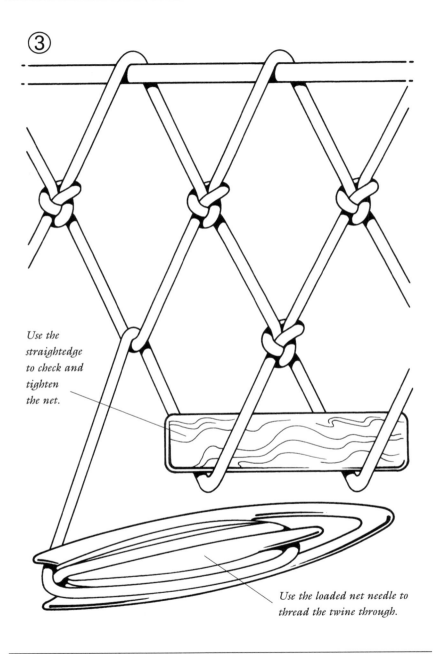

③

Use the
straightedge
to check and
tighten
the net.

Use the loaded net needle to
thread the twine through.

GLOSSARY

Astern. At or toward the rear part of a boat or the reversing maneuver of a vessel as in: *full speed astern!*

Belay. To secure a rope or line with figure-eight turns around a cleat.

Bend. The action of tying two ropes together by their ends. Also the name given to the group of knots that is used to tie lines to each other or to some other object.

Bight. The slack section of the rope between the working end and the standing end. The term is particularly used when this section of the rope is formed into a loop or turned back on itself. Knots tied "in the bight" or "on the bight" do not need the ends to be used in the tying process.

Bollard. A large fixed post made of iron or wood for mooring a boat to.

Bow. The front end of a boat.

Braid. To interweave several strands.

Breaking strength or **strain.** The manufacturer's estimate of the load that will cause a rope to part. This calculation is based on strength of a dry line under a steady pull; it generally takes no account of wetness, wear and tear, knots, or shock loading. Lines are weaker when worn, wet, or knotted and the manufacturer's estimate cannot, therefore, be regarded as a safe working load.

Cable. A rope of large diameter: anchor warp or chain.

Cable-laid. Rope formed of three right-handed hawsers laid up left-handed to make a larger, nine-stranded rope or cable.

Chafe. To make or become worn or frayed by rubbing.

Cleat. A T-shaped fitting on which a rope or line can be secured.

Cord. The name given to several tightly twisted yarns making a line with a diameter of less than one half inch.

Cordage. Collective name for ropes and cords, especially used to describe the ropes in a ship's rigging.

Core. The inner or central part found in ropes and sinnets of more than three strands, and in most braided lines. Formed from a bundle of parallel strands or loosely twisted yarn running the length of the rope, or the central part of a monkey's fist knot, inserted to add weight.

Eye. Loop formed at the end of a length of rope.

Fender. A cushion of flexible material positioned on the sides of boats to prevent damage when tying up or mooring.

Fid. Tapered wooden pin used to work or loosen strands of rope.

Fray. To unravel, especially the end of a piece of rope.

Heaving line. A line with a weighted knot tied at one end, that is attached to another heavier line and is thrown from boat to shore or to another vessel. The purpose of the line is to draw behind it a heavier line that will be used for tying up or mooring.

Grommet or **grummet.** A ring, usually made of metal or twisted rope, that is used to fasten the edge of a sail to its stay, hold an oar in place, etc.

Hawser. A rope or cable, five to twenty-four inches in circumference, large enough for towing or mooring.

Hitch. Knot made to secure a rope to a ring, spar, etc., or to another rope.

Lanyard. A short length of rope or cord made decorative with knots and sinnets. Used to secure personal objects; usually worn around the neck or attached to a belt.

Lay. The direction, right- or left-handed, of the twist in the strands that form a rope.

Line. Generic name for cordage with no specific purpose, although it can describe a particular use (clothesline, fishing line, etc.).

Loop. Part of a rope that is bent so that it comes together across itself.

Make fast. To secure a rope or line to a cleat, etc.

Nip. The binding pressure within a knot that stops it from slipping.

Plain-laid rope. Three-stranded rope laid (twisted) to the right.

Plait or **plat.** Pronounced *plat*. To intertwine strands in a pattern.

Port. The left-hand side of a boat looking forward.

Reeve. The act of threading or passing a rope through an aperture such as a ring, block, or cleat.

Running rigging. Rope or wire used to control the sails.

Seizing. To bind two ropes or cords together.

Sinnet or **sennet.** Braided cordage (flat, round, or square), formed from three to nine cords.

Small stuff. Thin cordage, twine, string, rope, or line that has a circumference of less than one inch, or a diameter of less than one half inch.

Spar. A mast, boom, or gaff.

Splice. To join the ends of rope by interweaving the strands.

Standing end. The short area at the end of the standing part of the rope.

Standing part. The part of the rope that is fixed and under tension (as opposed to the free working end with which the knot is tied).

Starboard. The right-hand side of a boat looking forward.

Stern. The back of a boat.

Stopper knot. Any terminal knot used to bind the end of a line, cord, or rope to prevent it from unraveling and also to provide a decorative end.

Strand. Yarns twisted together in the opposite direction to the yarn itself. Rope made from strands (rope that is not braided) is called laid line.

Taut. Tightly stretched.

Thimble. A metal or plastic eye used to shape an eye splice and prevent chafe.

Twine. Thin line of various types for various uses, as in whipping twine, etc.

Warp. A general term for mooring ropes, anchor cable, etc.

Whipping. Tightly wrapping small stuff around the end of a cord or rope to prevent it from fraying.

Work (to). To draw and shape a knot; to make the final arrangement.

Working end. The part of the rope or cord used actively in tying a knot. The opposite of the **standing end**.

Yarn. The basic element of rope or cord formed from artificial or synthetic filaments or natural fibers.

INDEX OF KNOTS